W. Lucas (William Lucas) Collins

Homer: The Odyssey

W. Lucas (William Lucas) Collins

Homer: The Odyssey

ISBN/EAN: 9783742857309

Manufactured in Europe, USA, Canada, Australia, Japa

Cover: Foto ©Andreas Hilbeck / pixelio.de

Manufactured and distributed by brebook publishing software (www.brebook.com)

W. Lucas (William Lucas) Collins

Homer: The Odyssey

A NEW AND CHEAPER EDITION.

THE ODYSSEY OF HOMER.

TRANSLATED INTO ENGLISH VERSE IN THE SPENSERIAN STANZA.

By PHILIP STANHOPE WORSLEY, M.A.

Third Edition, 2 vols. fcap. 8vo, 12s.

OPINIONS OF THE PRESS.

' But, meanwhile, Mr Worsley, applying the Spenserian stanza, that beautiful romantic measure, to the most romantic poem of the ancient world—making this stanza yield him, too (what it never yielded to Byron), its treasures of fluidity and sweet ease—above all, bringing to his taste a truly poetical sense and skill—has produced a version of the 'Odyssey' much the most pleasing of those hitherto produced, and which is delightful to read."—*Matthew Arnold.*

"If the translator has produced a work which, having caught the spirit of the poem, can delight those to whom the original is a sealed book, he can desire no higher praise: and this praise belongs justly to Mr Worsley. . . . He has placed in the hands of English readers a poem which deserves to outlive the present generation."—*Edinburgh Review.*

"We generally trace some thoughtful truth of detail in Mr Worsley's version, as well as truth of effect. . . . His translation exemplifies a quality of the Spenserian stanza which was long since established by Shenstone—its fitness for narrating incidents of extreme natural simplicity to a refined and fastidious age."—*Guardian.*

"We assign it, without hesitation, the first place among existing English translations."—*Westminster Review.*

"Mr Worsley's 'Odyssey,' which we are very glad to welcome in a new edition, and which has justly taken a high place among translations, is a very admirable example of what we prefer in an English version of Homer. No one supposes that Homer wrote in Spenserian stanza,—he certainly did not; but Mr Worsley's version of him in that metre would convey to English minds a far better idea of the beauty of the original than any effort to stretch the metre of an antique song on the rack of a language to which it is unsuited. Mr Worsley's 'Odyssey' is very delightful to read, or hear read aloud."—*Examiner.*

"We know of no translation of the Odyssey that is, in many passages, so attractive ; and though the Spenserian stanza has several marked disqualifications for the functions here required from it, there are some for which it is probably as well fitted as any metre which has been yet tried."—*Spectator.*

"Mr Worsley is unquestionably a great master of the Spenserian stanza, and of the stately diction which belongs to it. . . . He has contrived, especially in the descriptive portions, to give us some very striking reproductions of Homer's manner, and we have no hesitation in saying that we very much prefer his translation to any modern one that we have seen."—*John Bull.*

"This is the best Homeric translation in the English language."—*Weekly Review.*

WILLIAM BLACKWOOD & SONS, EDINBURGH AND LONDON.

CLASSICAL TRANSLATIONS.

THE ÆNEID OF VIRGIL. Translated in English Blank Verse by G. K. RICKARDS, M.A., and Lord RAVENSWORTH. 2 vols. fcap. 8vo, 10s.

"Lord Ravensworth's success and strength are to be found, not so much in his verbal force as in the Virgilian spirit which breathes throughout his lines. No English reader can well miss their poetical grace and vigour; no scholar will deem unfaithful the clean-cut, decisive lines of this masterly version."—*Evening Standard.*

THE METAMORPHOSES OF OVID. Translated in English Blank Verse. By HENRY KING, M.A., Fellow of Wadham College, Oxford, and of the Inner Temple, Barrister-at-Law. Crown 8vo, 10s. 6d.

"An excellent translation."—*Athenæum.*
"The execution is admirable. . . . It is but scant and inadequate praise to say of it that it is the best translation of the Metamorphoses that we have."—*Observer.*

THE ELEGIES OF ALBIUS TIBULLUS. Translated into English Verse, with Life of the Poet, and Illustrative Notes. By JAMES CRANSTOUN, LL.D., &c., Author of a Translation of 'Catullus.' In crown 8vo, 6s. 6d.

"We may congratulate Mr Cranstoun on having occupied a place for which his poetical skill, no less than his manifest classical training and acquirements, abundantly fits him."—*Saturday Review.*
"By far the best of the few versions we have of this sweet and graceful poet."—*Standard.*

THE ELEGIES OF SEXTUS PROPERTIUS. Translated into English Verse. By the SAME. In crown 8vo, 7s. 6d.

"In Mr Cranstoun's work free play is given to the poet's mood and tone at the time of writing, and a sound judgment is shown for the most part in the forms chosen to render passionate and pathetic love elegies, on the one hand, and archæological poems on Roman history and mythology, such as those of his later years, on the other. The result cannot fail to be a wider acquaintance with and appreciation of the Umbrian bard."—*Saturday Review.*

THE ODES, EPODES, AND SATIRES OF HORACE. Translated into English Verse, together with a Life of Horace, by THEODORE MARTIN. New Edition. Post 8vo, 9s.

THE POEMS OF CATULLUS. Translated into English Verse, with an Introduction and Notes. By the SAME. Second Edition, revised. Crown 8vo, printed on *papier vergé*, 7s. 6d.

POEMS AND TRANSLATIONS. By PHILIP STANHOPE WORSLEY, M.A., Fellow of Corpus Christi College, Oxford. Edited by Rev. EDWARD WORSLEY. New Edition, fcap. 8vo, 6s.

"Mr Worsley's poetry is always full of healthy spirit; he is tender as well as vigorous, and blends a deep religious spirit with classic grace."—*Saturday Review.*

WILLIAM BLACKWOOD & SONS, EDINBURGH AND LONDON.

ANCIENT CLASSICS FOR ENGLISH READERS

Edited by the Rev. W. LUCAS COLLINS, M.A.

In 20 Vols., crown 8vo, cloth, 2s. 6d. each.

And may also be had in 10 Volumes, neatly bound with calf or vellum back, price £2, 10s.

CONTENTS OF THE SERIES.

HOMER: THE ILIAD. By the EDITOR.
HOMER: THE ODYSSEY. By the EDITOR.
HERODOTUS. By GEORGE C. SWAYNE, M.A., late Fellow of Corpus Christi College, Oxford.
ÆSCHYLUS. By REGINALD S. COPLESTON, M.A., Fellow and Lecturer of St John's College, Oxford.
XENOPHON. By Sir ALEXANDER GRANT, Bart., Principal of the University of Edinburgh.
SOPHOCLES. By CLIFTON W. COLLINS, M.A., H.M. Inspector of Schools.
EURIPIDES. By W. B. DONNE.
ARISTOPHANES. By the EDITOR.
HESIOD AND THEOGNIS. By the Rev. J. DAVIS, M.A., late Scholar of Lincoln College, Oxford.
THE COMMENTARIES OF CÆSAR. By ANTHONY TROLLOPE.
VIRGIL. By the EDITOR.
HORACE. By THEODORE MARTIN.
CICERO. By the EDITOR.
PLINY'S LETTERS. By the Rev. ALFRED CHURCH, M.A., and the Rev. W. J. BRODRIBB, M.A.
JUVENAL. By EDWARD WALFORD, M.A., late Scholar of Balliol College, Oxford.
TACITUS. By W. B. DONNE.
LUCIAN. By the EDITOR.
PLAUTUS AND TERENCE. By the EDITOR.
PLATO. By CLIFTON W. COLLINS, M.A.
GREEK ANTHOLOGY. By LORD NEAVES, one of the Senators of the College of Justice in Scotland.

WILLIAM BLACKWOOD & SONS, EDINBURGH AND LONDON.

SUPPLEMENTARY SERIES.

ANCIENT CLASSICS
FOR
ENGLISH READERS.

Edited by the Rev. W. LUCAS COLLINS, M.A.

ADVERTISEMENT.

THE marked success and general popularity of the Series of "ANCIENT CLASSICS FOR ENGLISH READERS," lately concluded in twenty volumes, has been accompanied by some regrets, expressed both by the friendly critics of the press and in private quarters, at its not having been made somewhat more comprehensive.

This has induced us to announce the issue of a "Supplementary" Series, intended to comprise the works of some few Latin and Greek authors which, for various reasons, were not included in the original plan.

It is hoped that the whole collection will thus supply, in a popular and convenient form, such a view of the literature of Ancient Greece and Rome as may give a fair idea of its subject matter and its spirit to those who have not leisure to study it in the originals, and at the same time serve as an introduction to such study, where facilities for it can be enjoyed.

This Series will appear, like the preceding, in quarterly volumes, at half-a-crown each, and in the same size and type. It will not be extended beyond eight or ten such volumes. These will include the works of ARISTOTLE, THUCYDIDES, DEMOSTHENES, LIVY, LUCRETIUS, OVID, CATULLUS (with TIBULLUS and PROPERTIUS), ANACREON, PINDAR, &c.

WILLIAM BLACKWOOD AND SONS,
EDINBURGH AND LONDON.

Ancient Classics for English Readers

EDITED BY THE

REV. W. LUCAS COLLINS, M.A.

HOMER

THE ODYSSEY

HOMER

THE ODYSSEY

BY THE
REV. W. LUCAS COLLINS, M.A.
AUTHOR OF
'ETONIANA,' 'THE PUBLIC SCHOOLS,' ETC.

WILLIAM BLACKWOOD AND SONS
EDINBURGH AND LONDON
MDCCCLXXI

CONTENTS.

		PAGE
	INTRODUCTION,	1
CHAP. I.	PENELOPE AND HER SUITORS,	9
" II.	TELEMACHUS GOES IN QUEST OF HIS FATHER,	26
" III.	ULYSSES WITH CALYPSO AND THE PHÆACIANS,	43
" IV.	ULYSSES TELLS HIS STORY TO ALCINOUS,	65
" V.	THE TALE CONTINUED — THE VISIT TO THE SHADES,	78
" VI.	ULYSSES' RETURN TO ITHACA,	89
" VII.	THE RETURN OF TELEMACHUS FROM SPARTA,	95
" VIII.	ULYSSES REVISITS HIS PALACE,	100
" IX.	THE DAY OF RETRIBUTION,	109
" X.	THE RECOGNITION BY PENELOPE,	116
" XI.	CONCLUDING REMARKS,	125

It has been thought desirable in these pages to use the Latin names of the Homeric deities and heroes, as more familiar to English ears. As, however, most modern translators have followed Homer's Greek nomenclature, it may be convenient here to give both.

Zeus	=	Jupiter.
Herè	=	Juno.
Arēs	=	Mars.
Poseidōn	=	Neptune.
Pallas Athenè	=	Minerva.
Aphroditè	=	Venus.
Hephaistos	=	Vulcan.
Hermes	=	Mercury.
Artemis	=	Diana.
Odysseus	=	Ulysses.
Aias	=	Ajax.

The passages quoted, unless otherwise specified, are from the admirable translation of Mr Worsley.

INTRODUCTION.

The poem of the Odyssey is treated in these pages as the work of a single author, and that author the same as the composer of the Iliad. It would be manifestly out of place, in a volume which does not profess to be written for critical scholars, to discuss a question on which they are so far from being agreed. But it may be satisfactory to assure the reader who has neither leisure nor inclination to enter into the controversy, that in accepting, as we do, the Odyssey as from the same " Homer " to whom we owe the Tale of Troy, he may fortify himself by the authority of many accomplished scholars who have carefully examined the question. Though none of the incidents related in the Iliad are distinctly referred to in the Odyssey—a point strongly urged by those who would assign the poems to different authors—and therefore the one cannot fairly be regarded as a sequel to the other, yet there is no important discrepancy, either in the facts previously assumed, or in the treatment of such characters as appear upon the scene in both.

The character of the two poems is, indeed, essentially different. The Iliad is a tale of the camp and the battle-field: the Odyssey combines the romance of travel with that of domestic life. The key-note of the Iliad is glory: that of the Odyssey is rest. This was amongst the reasons which led one of the earliest of Homer's critics to the conclusion that the Odyssey was the work of his old age. In both poems the interest lies in the situations and the descriptions, rather than in what we moderns call the "plot." This latter is not a main consideration with the poet, and he has no hesitation in disclosing his catastrophe beforehand. The interest, so far as this point is concerned, is also weakened for the modern reader by the intervention throughout of supernatural agents, who, at the most critical turns of the story, throw their irresistible weight into the scale. Yet, in spite of this, the interest of the Odyssey is intensely human. Greek mythology and Oriental romance are large ingredients in the poem, but its men and women are drawn by a master's hand from the actual life; and, since in the two thousand years between our own and Homer's day nothing has changed so little as human nature, therefore very much of it is still a story of to-day.

The poem before us is the tale of the wanderings and adventures of Odysseus—or Ulysses, as the softer tongue of the Latins preferred to call him—on his way home from the siege of Troy to his island-kingdom of Ithaca. The name Odysseus has been variously interpreted. Homer himself, who should be the best authority, tells us that it was given to him by his grandfather Autolycus to signify "the child of hate." Others have interpreted it to mean "suffering;" and some ingenious scholars see in it only the ancient form of a familiar sobriquet by which the hero was known, "the little one," or "the dwarf,"—a conjecture which derives some support from the fact that the Tyrrhenians knew him under that designation. It may be remembered that in the Iliad he is described as bearing no comparison in stature with the stalwart forms of Agamemnon and Menelaus; and it is implied in the description that there was some want of proportion in his figure, since he appeared nobler than Menelaus when both sat down. But in the Odyssey itself there appears no reference to any natural defect of any kind. His character in this poem corresponds perfectly with that which is disclosed in the Iliad. There, he is the leading spirit of the Greeks when in council. Scarcely second to Achilles or Diomed in personal prowess, his advice and opinion are listened to with as much respect as those of the veteran Nestor. In the Iliad, too, he is, as he is called in the present poem, "the man of many devices." His accomplishments cover a larger field than those of any other hero. Achilles only can beat him in speed of foot; he is as good an archer as Ajax Oileus or Teucer; he throws Ajax the Great in the wrestling-match, in spite of his superior strength, by a happy use of science, and divides with him the prize of victory. To him, as the worthiest successor of Achilles—on the testimony of the Trojan prisoners, who declared that he had wrought them most harm of any—the armour of that great hero was awarded at his death. He is not tragic enough to fill the first place in the Iliad, but we are quite prepared to find him the hero of a story of travel and adventure like the Odyssey, in which the grand figure of Achilles would be entirely out of place.

The Odyssey has been pronounced, by a high classical authority, to be emphatically a lady's book. "The Iliad," says the great Bentley, "Homer made for men, and the Odyssey for the other sex." This opinion somewhat contradicts the criticism of an older and greater master—Aristotle—who defines the Odyssey as being "ethic and complex," while the Iliad is "pathetic and simple." Yet it was perhaps some such notion of the fitness of things which made Fénélon's adaptation of Homer's story, 'The Adventures of Telemachus in search of Ulysses,' so popular a French text-book in ladies' schools a century ago. It is certain, also, that the allusions in our modern literature, and the subjects of modern pictures, are drawn from the Odyssey even more frequently than from the Iliad, although the former has never been so generally read in our schools and colleges. Circe and the Sirens, Scylla and Charybdis, have pointed more morals than any incidents in the Siege of Troy. Turner's pictures of Nausicaa and her Maidens, the Gardens of Alcinous, the Cyclops addressed by Ulysses, the Song of the Sirens—all amongst our national heirlooms of art—assume a fair acquaintance with the later Homeric fable on the part of the public for whom they were painted. The secret of this greater popularity may lie in the fact, that while the adventures in the Odyssey have more of the romantic and the imaginative, the heroes are less heroic—have more of the common human type about them—than those of the Iliad. The colossal figure of Achilles in his wrath does not affect us so nearly as the wandering voyager with his strange adventures, his hairbreadth escapes, and his not over-scrupulous devices.

To our English sympathies the Odyssey appeals strongly for another reason—it is a tale of voyage and discovery. "It is," as Dean Alford says, "of all poems a poem of the sea." In the Iliad the poet never missed an opportunity of letting us know that—whoever he was and wherever he was born—he knew the sea well, and had a seaman's tastes. But there his tale confined him chiefly to the plain before Troy, and such opportunities presented themselves but rarely. In the Odyssey we roam from sea to sea throughout the narrative, and the restless hero seems never so much at home as when he is on shipboard. It is not without reason that the most ancient works of art which bear the figure of Ulysses represent him not as a warrior but as a sailor.

The Tale of Troy, as has been already said, embraces in its whole range three decades of years. It is with the last ten that the Odyssey has to do; and as in the Iliad, though the siege itself had consumed ten years, it is with the last year only that the poet deals; so in this second great poem also, the main action occupies no more than the last six weeks of the third and concluding decade.

Between the Iliad and the Odyssey there is an interval of events, not related in either poem, but which a Greek audience of the poet's own day would readily supply for themselves out of a store of current legend quite familiar to their minds, and embodied in more than one ancient poem now lost to us.* Troy, after the long siege, had fallen at last; but not to Achilles. For him the dying prophecy of Hector had been soon fulfilled, and an arrow from the bow of Paris had stretched him in death, like his noble enemy, " before the Scæan gates." It was his son Neoptolemus, " the red-haired," to whom the oracles pointed as the destined captor of the city. Ulysses went back to Greece to fetch him, and even handed over to the young hero, on his arrival, the armour of his father—his own much-valued prize. In that armour Neoptolemus led the Greeks to the storm and sack of the city by night, while the Trojans were either asleep or holding deep carousal.

It has been conjectured by some that, under the name of Ulysses, the poet has but described, with more or less of that licence to which he had a double claim as poet and as traveller, his own wanderings and adventures by land and sea. It has been argued, in a treatise of some ingenuity,† that the poet, whoever he was, was himself a native of the island in which he places the home of his hero. There is certainly one passage which reads very much like the circumstantial and loving description which a poet would give of his sea-girt birthplace, with every nook of which he would have been familiar from his childhood. It occurs in the scene where Ulysses is at last landed on the coast

* See Iliad, p. 143.
† Ulysses Homer; or, a Discovery of the True Author of the Iliad and Odyssey. By Constantine Koliades.

of Ithaca, which he is slow to recognise until his divine guide points out to him the different localities within sight :—

> "This is the port of sea-king Phorcys old,
> And this the olive at the haven's brow.
> Yonder the deep dark lovely cave behold,
> Shrine of the Naïad-nymphs! These shades enfold
> The stone-roofed bower, wherein thou oft hast stood,
> While to the Nymphs thy frequent vows uprolled,
> Steam of choice hecatombs and offerings good.
> Neritus hill stands there, high-crowned with waving wood." *

As conjecture only all such theories must remain; but it may at least be safely believed that the author had himself visited some of the strange lands which he describes, with whatever amount of fabulous ornament he may have enriched his tale, and it has a certain interest for the reader to entertain the possibility of a personal narrative thus underlying the romance.

* B. xiii. 345 (st. 45, Worsley).

THE ODYSSEY.

CHAPTER I.

PENELOPE AND HER SUITORS.

THE surviving heroes of the great expedition against Troy, after long wanderings, have at length reached their homes, with one exception — Ulysses has not been heard of in his island-kingdom of Ithaca. Ten years have nearly passed since the fall of Troy, and still his wife Penelope, and his aged father Laertes, and his young son Telemachus, now growing up to manhood, keep weary watch for the hero's return. There is, moreover, a twofold trouble in the house. It is not only anxiety for an absent husband, but the perplexity caused by a crowd of importunate suitors for her hand, which vexes the soul of Penelope from day to day. The young nobles of Ithaca and its dependent islands have for many years flocked to the palace to seek the hand of her whom they consider as virtually a widowed queen. It is to no purpose that she professes her own firm belief that Ulysses still survives: she has no kind of proof of his existence, and the suitors demand of her that—in accordance with what would appear the custom of the country—she shall make choice of some one among them to take the lost hero's place, and enjoy all the rights of sovereignty. How far the lovers were attracted by the wealth and position of the lady, and how far by the force of her personal charms, is a point somewhat hard to decide. The Roman poet Horace imputes to them the less romantic motive. They were, he says, of that class of prudent wooers—

> "Who prized good living more than ladies' love;"

and he even hints that Penelope's knowledge of their real sentiments helped to account for her obduracy. But Horace, we must remember, was a satirist by trade. A mere prosaic reader might be tempted to raise the question whether the personal charms of Penelope, irresistible as they might have been when Ulysses first left her for the war, must not have been somewhat impaired during the twenty years of his absence; and whether it was possible for a widow of that date (especially with a grown-up son continually present as a memento) to inspire such very ardent admiration. These arithmetical critics have always been the pests of poetry. One very painstaking antiquarian—Jacob Bryant—in the course of his studies on the Iliad, made the discovery, by a comparison of mythological dates, that Helen herself must have been nearly a hundred years old at the taking of Troy. But the question of age has been unanimously voted impertinent by all her modern admirers: she still shines in our fancy with

"The starlike beauty of immortal eyes"

which the Laureate saw in his 'Dream of Fair Women.' The heroic legends take no count of years. Woman is there beautiful by divine right of sex, unless in those few special instances in which, for the purposes of the story, particular persons are necessarily represented as old and decrepit. Nor is there any ground for supposing that the suitors of Penelope, like the courtiers of Queen Elizabeth, persisted in attributing to her fictitious charms. She is evidently not less beautiful in the poet's eyes than in theirs. As beauty has been happily said to be, after all, "the lover's gift," so also the bestowal of it upon whom he will must be allowed to be the privilege of the poet. The island-queen herself says, indeed, that her beauty had fled when Ulysses left her, and could only be restored by his return; but this disclaimer from the lips of a loving and mourning wife only makes her more charming, and she is not the only woman, ancient or modern, who has borrowed an additional fascination from her tears.

The suitors of Penelope, strange to say, are living at free quarters in the palace of the absent Ulysses. Telemachus is too young, apparently, to assert his rights as master of the house on his own or his mother's behalf. If the picture be true to the life—and there is no good reason to suppose it otherwise—

we must assume an age of rude licence even in the midst of considerable civilisation, when, unless a king or chief could hold his own by the strong hand, there was small chance of his rights being respected. A partial explanation may also lie in the fact that the wealth of the king was regarded as in some sort public property, and that to keep open house for all whose rank entitled them to sit at his table was probably a popular branch of the royal prerogative. Telemachus is an only son, and he and his mother have apparently no near kinsmen to avenge any wrong or insult that may be offered. There is, besides, somewhat of weakness and tameness in his character, more than befits the son of such a father. He is a home-nurtured youth, of a gentle and kindly nature, a dutiful and affectionate son; but his temperament is far too easy for the rude and troublous times in which his lot is cast, and the roystering crew who profess at least to be the wooers of Penelope have not been slow to find it out. Some kindly critics ("Christopher North" among the number) have refused to see any of these shortcomings in the young prince's character; but his father Ulysses saw them plainly. For thus it is he speaks, at a later period of the tale, under his disguise of a mendicant:—

> "Had I but youth as I have heart, or were
> The blameless brave Ulysses, or his son,
> Then let a stranger strike me headless there,
> If against any I leave revenge undone!"

But this is anticipating somewhat too much. We must return to the opening of the poem.

The fate of Ulysses, so far as any knowledge of it has reached his wife and son, lies yet in mystery. Only the gods know—and perhaps it were as well for Penelope not to know—in what unworthy thraldom he is held. He has incurred the anger of the great Sea-god, and therefore he is still forbidden to reach his home. He has lain captive now for seven long years in Ogygia, the enchanted realm of Calypso—

> "Girded of ocean in an island-keep,
> An island clothed with trees, the navel of the deep.
>
> "There dwells the child of Atlas, who can sound
> All seas, and eke doth hold the pillars tall
> Which keep the skies asunder from the ground.
> There him, still sorrowing, she doth aye enthral,
> Weaving serene enticements to forestal
> The memory of his island-realm."

But the goddess of wisdom, who was his protecting genius throughout the perils of the great siege, and by whose aid, as we have seen in the Iliad, he has distanced so many formidable competitors in the race for glory, has not forgotten her favourite. The opening scene of the Odyssey shows us the gods in council on Olympus. Neptune alone is absent; he is gone to feast, like Jupiter in the Iliad, with those mysterious people, the far-off Æthiopians—

> "Extreme of men, who diverse ways retire,
> Some to the setting, some the rising sun."

Minerva takes the opportunity of his absence to remind the Father of the gods of the hard fate of Ulysses, so unworthy of a hero who has deserved so well both of gods and men. It is agreed to send Mercury, the messenger of the Immortals, to the island where Calypso holds Ulysses captive in her toils, to announce to him that the day of his return draws near. Minerva herself, meanwhile, will go to Ithaca, and put strength into the heart of his son Telemachus, that he may rid his house of this hateful brood of revellers, and set forth to make search for his father. The passage in which the poet describes her visit is a fine one, and it has been finely rendered by Mr Worsley:—

> "So ending, underneath her feet she bound
> Her faery sandals of ambrosial gold,
> Which o'er the waters and the solid ground
> Swifter than wind have borne her from of old;
> Then on the iron-pointed spear laid hold,
> Heavy and tall, wherewith she smites the brood
> Of heroes till her anger waxes cold;
> Then from Olympus swept in eager mood,
> And with the island-people in the court she stood

> "Fast by the threshold of the outer gate
> Of brave Odysseus: in her hand she bore
> The iron-pointed spear, heavy and great,
> And, waiting as a guest-friend at the door,
> Of Mentes, Taphian chief, the likeness wore;
> There found the suitors, who beguiled with play
> The hours, and sat the palace-gates before
> On hides of oxen which themselves did slay—
> Haughty of mien they sat, and girt with proud array."

As the young prince sits thus, an unwilling host in his father's hall, meditating, says the poet, whether or no some day that father may return suddenly and take vengeance on these invaders of his rights, against whom he himself seems powerless, he lifts his eyes

and sees a stranger standing at the gate. With simple
and high-bred courtesy—the courtesy of the old Bible
patriarchs, and even now practised by the Orientals,
though the march of modern civilisation has left little
remnant of it in our western isles—he hastes to bid
the stranger welcome, on the simple ground that he is
a stranger, and will hear no word of his errand until
the rights of hospitality have been paid. Eager as he
is to hear possible news of his father, he restrains his
anxiety to question his guest. Not until the handmaidens have brought water in the silver ewers, and
the herald, and the carver, and the dame of the pantry
(it is a right royal establishment, if somewhat rude)
have each done their office to supply the stranger's
wants, does Telemachus ask him a single question.
But when the suitors have ended their feast, they call
for music and song. They compel Phemius, the household bard, to make mirth for them. Then, while he
plies his voice and lyre for their entertainment, the
son of Ulysses whispers aside with his visitor. Who
is he, and whence does he come? Is he a friend of
his father's? For many a guest, and none unwelcome,
had come to those halls, as the son well knows, in *his*
day. Above all, does he bring news of *him?* Then
the disguised goddess tells her story, with a circumstantial minuteness of invention which befits wisdom when
she condescends to falsehood :—

"Know, my name is hight
Mentes, the son of brave Anchialus,
And sea-famed Taphos is my regal right;
And with my comrades am I come to-night

> Hither, in sailing o'er the wine-dark sea
> To men far off, who stranger tongues indite.
> For copper am I bound to Temesè,
> And in my bark I bring sword-steel along with me.

> "Moored is my ship beyond the city walls,
> Under the wooded cape, within the bay.
> We twain do boast, each in the other's halls,
> Our fathers' friendship from an ancient day.
> Hero Laertes ask, and he will say."

But of Ulysses' present fate the guest declares he knows nothing; only he has a presentiment that he is detained somewhere in an unwilling captivity, but that, "though he be bound with chains of iron," he will surely find his way home again. But in any case, as his father's friend, the supposed Mentes bids Telemachus take heart and courage, and act manfully for himself. Let him give this train of riotous suitors fair warning to quit the palace, and waste his substance no more; let his mother Penelope go back to her own father's house (if she desires to wed again), and make her choice and hold her wedding-banquet there; and for his own part, let him at once set sail and make inquiry for his father round the coasts of Greece. It may be that Nestor of Pylos, or Menelaus of Sparta— the last returned of the chiefs of the expedition—can give him some tidings. If he can only hear that Ulysses is yet alive, then he may well endure to wait his return with patience; if assured of his death, it will befit him to take due vengeance on these his enemies. The divine visitor even hints a reproach of Telemachus' present inactivity:—

"No more, with thews like these, to weakness cling.
Hast thou not heard divine Orestes' fame,
Who slew the secret slayer of the king
His father, and achieved a noble name?
Thou also, friend, to thine own strength lay claim—
Comely thou art and tall—that men may speak
Thy prowess, and their children speak the same."

The young prince duteously accepts the counsel, as from his father's friend, and prays his guest to tarry a while. But Minerva, her mission accomplished, suddenly changes her shape, spreads wings, and vanishes. Then Telemachus recognises the goddess, and feels a new life and spirit born within him. If we choose to admit an allegorical interpretation—more than commonly tempting, as must be confessed, in this particular case—it is the advent of Wisdom and Discretion to the conscious heart of the youth, hitherto too little awakened to its responsibilities.

Telemachus returns to his place among the revellers a new man. They are still listening to the minstrel, Phemius, who chants a lay of the return of the Greek chiefs from Troy, and the sufferings inflicted on them during their homeward voyage by the vengeance of the gods. The sound reaches Penelope where she sits apart with her wise maidens, like the mother of Sisera, in her "upper chamber"—the "bower" of the ladies of mediæval chivalry. She comes down the stair, and stands on the threshold of the banqueting-hall, attracted by the song. But the subject is too painful. She calls the bard to her, and begs him, for her sake, to choose some other theme. We must not be too angry with Telemachus because, in the first flush of his newly-awakened sense of the responsibilities of his position, he uses language, in addressing his mother, which to our ears has a sound of harshness and reproach. He bids her not presume to set limits to the inspiration of the bard—the noblest theme is ever the best. He reminds her that woman's kingdom is the loom and the distaff, and that the rule over men in his father's house now belongs to him. Viewed with reference to the tone of the age as regarded the duties of women,—compared with the parting charge of Hector in the Iliad to the wife he loved so tenderly, and even with a higher example in Scripture,—there is nothing startling or repulsive in such language from a son to his mother. To the young prince in his new mood, while the counsels of Minerva were yet ringing in his ears, the absence and the sufferings of his father might well seem the only theme on which he could endure to hear the minstrel descant; it was of this, he feels, that he needed to be continually reminded. And if hitherto he has allowed this riotous company to assume that, in the absence of Ulysses, the government of his house has rested in the weak hands of a woman, it shall be so no longer. He will take his father's place.

The mother sees the change in her son's temper with some surprise—we may suppose, with somewhat mingled feelings of approval and mortification. The boy has grown into a man on the sudden. The poet gives us but a single word as any clue to the effect upon Penelope of this evidently unaccustomed outburst of self-assertion on the part of Telemachus. "Astonished," he says, she withdraws at once to her

upper chamber, and there weeps her sorrows to sleep.
Telemachus himself addresses the assembled company
in a tone which is evidently as new to their ears as to
those of his mother. He bids them, with a haughty
courtesy, feast their fill to-night; to-morrow he will
summon (as is the custom of the Homeric princes) a
council of the heads of the people, and there he will
give them all public warning to quit his father's house,
and feast—if they needs must feast—in each other's
houses, at their own cost. If they refuse, and still
make this riot of an absent man's wealth, he appeals
from men to "the gods who live for ever" for a sure
and speedy vengeance.

The careless revellers mark the change in the young
man as instantly as Penelope. For a few moments
they bite their lips in silence—"wondering that he
spake so bold." The first to answer him is Antinous,
the most prominent ringleader of the confraternity of
suitors. His character is very like that of the worst
stamp of the "Cavalier" of the days of our own Charles
II. Brave, bold, and insolent, there is yet a reckless
gaiety and a ready wit about him which would have
made him at once a favourite in that unprincipled
court. He adds to these characteristics a quality of
which he might, unhappily, have also found a high
example there—that of ingratitude. He is bound by
strong ties of obligation to the house of Ulysses; his
father had come in former days to seek an asylum with
the Chief of Ithaca from the vengeance of the Thesprotians, and had been kindly entertained by him
until his death. The son now answers Telemachus

with a taunting compliment upon the new character in which he has just come out. "He means to claim for himself the sovereignty of the island, as his father's heir, no doubt; but the gods forbid that Ithaca should ever come under the rule of so fierce a despot!" Telemachus makes answer that he will at all events rule his father's house. Upon this, Eurynomus, another leading spirit among the rivals—a smoother-tongued and more cautious individual—soothes the angry youth with what seems a plausible recognition of his rights, in order that he may get an answer to a question on which he feels an interest not unmixed, as we may easily understand, with some secret apprehension. "Who was this traveller from over sea? and—did he happen to bring any news of Ulysses?" But Telemachus has learnt subtlety as well as wisdom from the disguised goddess. He gives the name assumed by his visitor, Mentes, an old friend of the house. But as to his father's return, the oracles of the gods and the reports of men all agree in pronouncing it to have now become hopeless. So the revel is renewed till nightfall; and while the feasters go off to their own quarters somewhere near at hand, Telemachus retires to his chamber (separate, apparently, from the main building), where his old nurse Eurycleia tends him with a careful affection, as though he were still a child, folding and hanging up the vest of fine linen which he takes off when he lies down to sleep, and drawing the bolt of the chamber door through its silver ring when she leaves him.

The council of notables is summoned for the morrow.

No such meeting has been held since the departure of Ulysses for Troy. As Telemachus passes to take his place there, all men remark a new majesty in his looks.

> "So when the concourse to the full was grown,
> He lifted in his hand the steely spear,
> And to the council moved, but not alone,
> For as he walked his swift dogs followed near.
> Also Minerva did with grace endear
> His form, that all the people gazed intent
> And wondered, while he passed without a peer.
> Straight to his father's seat his course he bent,
> And the old men gave way in reverence as he went."

He makes his passionate protest before them all against the insufferable waste of his household by this crew of revellers, and against their own supineness in offering him no aid to dislodge them. Antinous rises to answer him, beginning, as before, with an ironical compliment—"the young orator's language is as sublime as his spirit." But the fault, he begs to assure him, lies not with the suitors, but with the queen herself. She has been playing fast and loose with her lovers, deluding them, for these three years past, with vain hopes and false promises. She had, indeed, been practising a kind of pious fraud upon them. She had set up a mighty loom, in which she wrought diligently to complete, as she professed, a winding-sheet of delicate texture for her husband's father, the aged Laertes, against the day of his death. Not until this sad task was finished, she entreated of them, let her be asked to choose a new bridegroom. To so much forbearance they had all assented; but lo! they had lately discovered that what she wrought by day she carefully unwound by night, so that the task promised to be an endless one. Some of the handmaidens (who had found their own lovers, too, amongst their royal mistress's many suitors) had betrayed her secret. Antinous is gallant enough to add to this recital of Penelope's craft warm praises of the queen herself, even giving her full credit for the bright woman's wit which had so long baffled them all.

> "Matchless skill
> To weave the splendid web ; sagacious thought,
> And shrewdness such as never fame ascribed
> To any beauteous Greek of ancient days,
> Tyro, Mycene, or Alcmene, loved
> Of Jove himself, all whom th' accomplished queen.
> Transcends in knowledge—ignorant alone
> That, wooed long time, she should at last be won."—(Cowper.)

But they will now be put off no longer—she must make her choice, or they will never leave the house so long as she remains there unespoused. Telemachus indignantly refuses to send his mother home to her father ; and repeats his passionate appeal to the gods for vengeance against the wrongs which he is himself helpless to deal with. At once an omen from heaven seems to betoken that the appeal is heard and accepted. Two eagles are seen flying over the heads of the crowd assembled in the marketplace, where they suddenly wheel round, and tear each other furiously with beak and talons. The soothsayer is at hand to interpret ; the aged Halitherses, who reminds them all how he had foretold, when Ulysses first left his own shores for Troy, the twenty years that would elapse before his return. Now, he sees by this portent, the happy day is near at hand; nay, in his zeal for his master's house he goes so far as to urge the assembled people to take upon themselves at once the punishment of these traitors. One of the suitors mocks at the old man's auguries, and threatens him for his interference. The prophet is silenced; and Telemachus, finding no support from the assembly, asks but for a ship and crew to be furnished him, that he may set forth in search of his father. One indignant voice, among the apathetic crowd, is raised in the young prince's defence: it is that of Mentor, to whom Ulysses had intrusted the guardianship of his rights in his absence. His name has passed into a synonym for all prudent guardians and moral counsellors, chiefly in consequence of Fénélon's didactic tale of 'Télémaque,' already mentioned, in which the adventures of the son of Ulysses were "improved," with elaborate morals, for the benefit of youth; and in which Mentor, as the young prince's travelling tutor, played a conspicuous part. He vents his indignation here in a very striking protest against popular ingratitude:—

> "Hear me, ye Ithacans;—be never king
> From this time forth benevolent, humane,
> Or righteous; but let every sceptred hand
> Rule merciless, and deal in wrong alone;
> Since none of all his people, whom he swayed
> With such paternal gentleness and love,
> Remembers the divine Ulysses more."—(Cowper.)

He, too, meets with jeers and mockery from the insolent nobles, and Telemachus quits the assembly to wander in melancholy mood along the sea-shore—the usual resort, it will be remarked, of the Homeric heroes, when they seek to calm the tumult of grief or anger. Such appeal to the soothing influence of what Homer calls the "illimitable" ocean is not less true to nature than it is characteristic of the poetical and imaginative temperament. Bathing his hands in the sea waves—for prayer, to the Greek as to the Hebrew mind, demanded a preparatory purification—Telemachus lifts his cry to his guardian goddess, Minerva. At once she stands before him there in the likeness of Mentor. She speaks to him words of encouragement and counsel. Evil men may mock at him now; but if he be determined to prove himself the true son of such a father, he shall not lack honour in the end. She will provide him ship and crew for his voyage. Thus encouraged by the divine Wisdom which speaks in the person of Mentor, he returns to the banquet-hall, to avoid suspicion. Yet, when Antinous greets him there with a mocking show of friendship, he wrenches his hand roughly from his grasp, and quits the company. Taking into his counsels his nurse Eurycleia—who is the palace housekeeper also—he bids her make ready good store of provisions for his voyage: twelve capacious vessels filled with the ripest wine, twenty measures of fine meal, and grain besides, carefully sewn up in wallets. In the dusk of this very evening, unknown to his mother, he will embark; for the goddess (still in Mentor's likeness) has chartered for him a galley with twenty stout rowers, which is to lie ready launched for him in the harbour at nightfall. Eurycleia vainly remonstrates with her nursling on his dangerous purpose—

> "'Ah! bide with thine own people here at ease.
> There is no call to suffer useless pain,
> Wandering always on the barren seas.'
> But he : 'Good nurse, prithee take heart again,
> These things are not without a god nor vain.
> Swear only that my mother shall not know
> Till twelve days pass, or she herself be fain
> To ask thee, or some other the tidings show,
> Lest her salt tears despoil much loveliness with woe.'"

Telemachus's resolve is fixed. As soon as the shadows of evening fall, Minerva sends a strange drowsiness on the assembled revellers in the hall of Ulysses, so that the wine-cups drop from their hands, and they stagger off early to their couches. Then, in the person of Mentor, she summons Telemachus to where the galley lies waiting for him, guides him on board, and takes her place beside him in the stern.

> "Loud and clear
> Sang the bluff Zephyr o'er the wine-dark mere
> Behind them. By Athene's hest he blew.
> Telemachus his comrades on did cheer
> To set the tackling. With good hearts the crew
> Heard him, and all things ranged in goodly order true.

> "The olive mast, planted with care, they bind
> With ropes, the white sails stretch on twisted hide,
> And brace the mainsail to the bellying wind.
> Loudly the keel rushed through the seething tide.
> Soon as the good ship's gear was all applied,
> They ranged forth bowls crowned with dark wine, and poured
> To gods who everlastingly abide,
> Most to the stern-eyed child of heaven's great lord.
> All night the ship clave onward till the Dawn upsoared."

CHAPTER II.

TELEMACHUS GOES IN QUEST OF HIS FATHER.

HITHERTO, and throughout the first four books of the poem, Telemachus, and not Ulysses, is the hero of the tale. The voyagers soon reach the rocky shores of Pylos,* the stronghold of the old "horse-tamer," Nestor. He has survived the long campaign in which so many of his younger comrades fell, and is now sitting, surrounded by his sons, at a great public banquet held in honour of the Sea-god. Telemachus, with a natural modesty not unbecoming his youth, is at first reluctant to accost and question a chieftain so full of years and renown, and his attendant guardian has to reassure him by the promise that "heaven will put words into his mouth." There is no need of question yet, however, either on the side of hosts or guests. Pisistratus, the youngest son of Nestor, upon whom the duties of "guest-master" naturally fall, welcomes the travellers with the invariable courtesy accorded by the laws of Homeric society to all strangers as their right, bids them take a seat at the banquet, and proffers the wine-

* Probably the modern Coryphasium.

cup—to the supposed Mentor first, as the elder. He only requests of them, before they drink, to join their hosts in their public supplication to Neptune; for he will not do them the injustice to suppose prayer can be unknown or distasteful to them, be they who they may—"All men have need of prayer." When the prayer has been duly made by both for a blessing on their hosts and for their own safe return, and when they have eaten and drunk to their hearts' content, then, and not till then, Nestor inquires their errand. The form in which the old chief put his question is as strongly characteristic of a primitive civilisation as the open hospitality which has preceded it. He asks the voyagers, in so many words, whether they are pirates? —not for a moment implying that such an occupation would be to their discredit. The freebooters of the sea in the Homeric times were dangerous enough, but not disreputable. It was an iron age, when every man's hand was more or less against his neighbour, and the guest of to-day might be an enemy to-morrow. Nestor's downright question may help a modern reader to understand the waste of Ulysses' substance in his absence by the lawless spirits of Ithaca. It was only so long as "the strong man armed kept his palace" in person that his goods were in peace. Telemachus, in reply, declares his name and errand, and implores the old chieftain, in remembrance of the days when he and Ulysses fought side by side at Troy, to give him, if he can, some tidings of his father.

"Answered him Nestor, the Gerenian knight:
'Friend, thou remind'st me of exceeding pain,

> Which we, the Achaians of unconquered might,
> There, and in ships along the clouded main,
> Led by Achilleus to the spoil, did drain,
> With those our fightings round the fortress high
> Of Priam king. There all our best were slain—
> There the brave Aias and Achilleus lie;
> Patroclus there, whose wisdom matched the gods on high.
>
> "'There too Antilochus my son doth sleep,
> Who in his strength was all so void of blame—
> Swift runner, and staunch warrior.'"

Nestor shows the same love of story-telling which marks his character in the Iliad. Modern critics who are inclined to accuse the old chief of garrulity should remember that, in an age in which there were no daily newspapers with their "special correspondents," a good memory and a fluent tongue were very desirable qualifications of old age. The old campaigner in his retirement was the historian of his own times. Unless he told his story often and at length amongst the men of a younger generation when they met at the banquet, all memory of the gallant deeds of old would be lost, and even the professional bard would have lacked the data on which to build his lay. Many a Nestor must have been ready—in season and out of season—to

> "Shoulder his crutch, and show how fields were won,"

before any Homer could have sung of the Trojan war. Even now, we are ready to listen readily to the veteran's reminiscences of a past generation, whether in war or peace, who has a retentive memory and a pleasant style—only he now commonly tells his story in print.

Nestor proceeds to tell his guests how the gods, after Troy was taken, had stirred up strife between

the brother-kings Agamemnon and Menelaus; and
how, in consequence, the fleet had divided, Menelaus
with one division sailing straight for home, while the
rest had waited with Agamemnon in the hope of ap-
peasing the wrath of heaven. Ulysses, who had at
first set sail with Menelaus, had turned back and re-
joined his leader. Of his subsequent fate Nestor
knows nothing; but he bids the young man take
courage. He has heard of the troubles that beset him
at home; but if Minerva vouchsafes to the son the
love and favour which (as was known to all the Greeks)
she bore to his father, all will go well with him yet.
Neither Nestor nor Telemachus are aware (though the
reader is) that the Wisdom which had made Ulysses a
great name was even now guiding the steps of his son.
One thing yet the youth longs to hear from the lips of
his father's ancient friend—the terrible story of Agamemnon's death by the hands of his wife and her paramour, and the vengeance taken by his son Orestes. It
is a tale which he has heard as yet but darkly, but has
dwelt upon in his heart ever since the goddess, at her
visit under the shape of Mentes, made such significant
reference to the story. Nestor tells it now at length—
the bloody legend which, variously shaped, became the
theme of the poet and the dramatist from generation
to generation of Greek literature. In Homer's version
we miss some of the horrors which later writers wove
into the tale; and it is not unlikely that, in the simpler
form in which it is here given, we have the main facts
of an actual domestic tragedy. During Agamemnon's
long absence in the Trojan war, his queen Clytemnes-

tra, sister of Helen, had been seduced from her marriage faith by her husband's cousin Ægisthus. In vain had the household bard, faithful to the trust committed to him by his lord in his absence, counselled and warned his lady against the peril; and Ægisthus at last, hopeless of his object so long as she had these honest eyes upon her, had caused him to be carried to a desert island to perish with hunger. So she fell, and Ægisthus ruled palace and kingdom. At last Agamemnon returned from the weary siege, and, landing on the shore of his kingdom, knelt down and kissed the soil in a transport of joyful tears. It is probably with no conscious imitation, but merely from the correspondence of the poet's mind, that Shakespeare attributes the very same expression of feeling to his Richard II. :—

> "I weep for joy
> To stand upon my kingdom once again.
> Dear earth, I do salute thee with my hand,
> Though rebels wound thee with their horses' hoofs :
> As a long-parted mother with her child
> Plays fondly with her tears, and smiles in meeting,
> So weeping, smiling, greet I thee, my earth,
> And do thee favour with my royal hands."

Agamemnon meets with as tragical a reception from the usurper of his rights as did Richard Plantagenet :—

> "Many the warm tears from his eyelids shed,
>   When through the mist of his long-hoped delight
>   He saw the lovely land before him spread.
>   Him from high watch-tower marked the watchman wight
>   Set by Ægisthus to watch day and night,
>   Two talents of pure gold his promised hire.
>   Twelve months he watched, lest the Avenger light
>   Unheeded, and remember his old fire ;
> Then to his lord made haste to show the tidings dire.

> "Forthwith Ægisthus, shaping a dark snare,
> Score of his bravest chose, and ambush set,
> And bade rich banquets close at hand prepare.
> Then he with horses and with chariots met
> The king, and welcomed him with fair words, yet
> With fraud at heart, and to the feast him led;
> There, like a stalled ox, smote him while he fed."

For seven years the adulterer and usurper reigned in security at Mycenæ. But meanwhile the boy Orestes, stolen away from the guilty court by his elder sister, was growing up to manhood, the destined avenger of blood, at Athens. In the seventh year he came back in disguise to his father's house, slew Ægisthus, and recovered his inheritance. There was a darker shadow still thrown over Agamemnon's death by later poets, which finds no place in Homer. The tragic interest in the dramas of Æschylus and Sophocles, which are founded on this story, lies in their representing Clytemnestra herself as the murderess of her husband, and Orestes, as his father's avenger, not hesitating to become the executioner of his mother as well as of her paramour.

Nestor has finished his story, and the travellers offer to return to their vessel and continue their quest; but the old chieftain will not hear of it. That night, at least, they must remain as his guests—on the morrow he will send them on to the court of Menelaus at Sparta, where they may chance to learn the latest tidings of Ulysses. Telemachus's guardian bids him accept the invitation, then suddenly spreads wings, and takes to flight in the likeness of a sea-eagle; and both Nestor and Telemachus recognise at last that, in the shape of Mentor, the goddess of wisdom has been so long his guide. A sacrifice is forthwith offered in her honour—a heifer, with horns overlaid with gold; a public banquet is held as before, and then, according to promise, Telemachus is sped on his journey. A pair of swift and strong-limbed horses—the old chief knew what a good horse was, and charged his sons specially to take the best in his stalls—are harnessed for the journey, and good provision of corn and wine, "such as was fit for princes," stored in the chariot. Pisistratus himself mounts beside his new friend as driver. Their first day's stage is Pheræ, where they are hospitably entertained by Nestor's friend, Diocles; and, after driving all the following day, they reach the palace gates of Menelaus, in Sparta, when the sun has set upon the yellow harvest fields, "and all the ways are dim."

At Sparta, too, as at Pylos, the city is holding high festival on the evening of their arrival. A double marriage is being celebrated in the halls of Menelaus. Hermione, his sole child by Helen, is leaving her parents to become the bride of Neoptolemus (otherwise known as Pyrrhus, the "red-haired"), son of the great Achilles; and at the same time the young Megapenthes, Menelaus's son by a slave wife, is to be married in his father's house. There is music and dancing in the halls when the travellers arrive; but Menelaus, like Nestor, will ask no questions of the strangers until the bath, and food, and wine in plenty, have refreshed them, and their horses have good barley-meal and rye set before them in the mangers. The magnificence of

Menelaus's palace, as described by the poet, is a very remarkable feature in the tale. It reads far more like a scene from the 'Arabian Nights' than a lay of early Greece. The lofty roofs fling back a flashing light as the travellers enter, "like as the splendour of the sun or moon." Gold, silver, bronze, ivory, and electrum, combine their brilliancy in the decorations. The guests wash in lavers of silver, and the water is poured from golden ewers. Telemachus is struck with wonder at the sight, and can compare it to nothing earthly.

> "Such and so glorious to celestial eyne
> Haply may gleam the Olympian halls divine!"

The palaces of Sparta, as seen in Homer's vision, contrast remarkably with the estimate formed of them by the Greek historian of a later age. Thucydides speaks of the city as having no public buildings of any magnificence, such as would impress a stranger with an idea of its real power, but wearing rather the appearance of a collection of villages. It is difficult to conceive that the actual Sparta of a much earlier age could have contained anything at all corresponding to this Homeric ideal of splendour; and the question arises, whether we have here an indistinct record of an earlier and extinct civilisation, or whether the poet drew an imaginary description from his own recollections of the gorgeous barbaric splendour of some city in the further East, which he had visited in his travels. If this be nothing more than a poet's exaggerated and idealised view of an actual state of higher civilisation, which once really existed in the old Greek kingdoms, and disappeared under the Dorian Heraclids, it is a singular record of a backward step in a nation's history; and the Homeric poems become especially valuable as preserving the memorials of a state of society which would otherwise have passed altogether into oblivion. There is less difficulty in believing the possible existence of an ante-historical civilisation which afterwards became extinct, if we remember the splendours of Solomon's court, as to which the widespread traditions of the East only corroborate the records of Scripture, and all which passed away almost entirely with its founder. It is remarkable that in the ancient Welsh poem, 'Y Gododin,' by Aneurin Owen, of which the supposed date is A.D. 570, there are very similar properties and scenery: knights in "armour of gold" and "purple plumes," mounted on "thick-maned chargers," with "golden spurs," who must—if ever they rode the Cambrian mountains—have been a very different race from the wild Welsh who held Edward Longshanks at bay. Are we to look upon this as merely the common language of all poets? and, if so, how comes it to be common to all? Were the Welsh who fought in the half-mythical battle of Cattraeth as far superior, in the scale of civilisation, to their successors who fell at Conway, as the Spartans under Menelaus (if Homer's picture of them is to be trusted) were to the Spartans under Leonidas? or was there some remote original, Oriental or other, whence this ornate military imagery passed into the poetry of such very different nations?

So, too, when Helen—now restored to her place in Menelaus's household—comes forth to greet the strangers, her whole surroundings are rather those of an Eastern sultana than of any princess of Spartan race.

> " Forth from her fragrant chamber Helen passed
> Like gold-bowed Dian : and Adraste came
> The bearer of her throne's majestic frame ;
> Her carpet's fine-wrought fleece Alcippe bore,
> Phylo her basket bright with silver ore,
> Gift of the wife of Polybus, who swayed
> When Thebes, the Egyptian Thebes, scant wealth displayed.
> His wife Alcandra, from her treasured store,
> A golden spindle to fair Helen bore,
> And a bright silver basket, on whose round
> A rim of burnished gold was closely bound."—(Sotheby.)

These elaborate preparations for her "work"—which is some delicate fabric of wool tinged with the costly purple dye—have little in common with the household loom of Penelope. Here, as in the Iliad, refinement and elegance of taste are the distinctive characteristics of Helen; and they help to explain, though they in no way excuse, the fascination exercised over her by Paris, the accomplished musician and brilliant converser, rich in all the graces which Venus, for her own evil purposes, had bestowed on her favourite. Helen is still, as in the Iliad, emphatically "the lady;" the lady of rank and fashion, as things were in that day, with all the fashionable faults, and all the fashionable good qualities: selfish and luxurious, gracious and fascinating. Her transgressions, and the seemingly lenient view which the poet takes of them, have been discussed sufficiently in the Iliad. They are all now condoned. She has recovered from her miserable infatuation ; and if we are inclined to despise Menelaus for his easy temper as a husband, we must remember the mediæval legends of Arthur and Guinevere, to whom Helen bears, in many points of character, a strong resemblance. The readiness which Arthur shows to have accepted at any time the repentance of his queen is almost repulsive to modern feeling, but was evidently not so to the taste of the age in which those legends were popular; nor is it at all clear that such forgiveness is less consonant with the purest code of morality than the stern implacability towards such offences which the laws of modern society would enjoin. Menelaus has forgiven Helen, even as Arthur—though not Mr Tennyson's Arthur—would have forgiven Guinevere. But she has not forgiven herself, and this is a strong redeeming point in her character; "shameless" is still the uncompromising epithet which she applies to herself, as in the Iliad, even in the presence of her husband and his guests.

They, too, have been wanderers since the fall of Troy, like the lost Ulysses. The king tells his own story before he interrogates his guest :—

> " Hardly I came at last, in the eighth year,
> Home with my ships from my long wanderings.
> Far as to Cyprus in my woe severe,
> Phœnice, Egypt, did the waves me bear.
> Sidon and Ethiopia I have seen,
> Even to Erembus roamed, and Libya, where
> The lambs are full-horned from their birth, I ween,
> And in the rolling year the fruitful flocks thrice yean."

He has grown rich in his travels, and would be happy, but for the thought of his brother Agamemnon's miserable end. Another grief, too, lies very close to his heart—the uncertainty which still shrouds the fate of his good comrade Ulysses.

> " His was the fate to suffer grievous woe,
> And mine to mourn without forgetfulness,
> While onward and still on the seasons flow,
> And he yet absent, and I comfortless.
> Whether he live or die we cannot guess.
> Him haply old Laertes doth lament,
> And sage Penelope, in sore distress,
> And to Telemachus the hours are spent
> In sadness, whom he left new-born when first he went."

The son is touched at the reminiscence, and drops a quiet tear, while for a moment he covers his eyes with his robe. It is at this juncture that Helen enters the hall. Her quick thought seizes the truth at once; as she had detected the father through his disguise of rags when he came as a spy into Troy, so now she recognises the son at once by his strong personal resemblance. Then Menelaus, too, sees the likeness, and connects it with the youth's late emotion. Young Pisistratus at once tells him who his friend is, and on what errand they are travelling together. Warm is the greeting which the King of Sparta bestows on the son of his old friend. There shall be no more lamentation for this night; all painful subjects shall be at least postponed until the morrow. But still, as the feast goes on, the talk is of Ulysses. Helen has learnt, too, in her wanderings, some of the secrets of Egyptian pharmacy. She has mixed in the wine a potent Eastern drug, which raises the soul above all care and sorrow—

"Which so cures heartache and the inward stings,
That men forget all sorrow wherein they pine.
He who hath tasted of the draught divine
Weeps not that day, although his mother die
Or father, or cut off before his eyes
Brother or child beloved fall miserably,
Hewn by the pitiless sword, he sitting silent by."

The "Nepenthes" of Helen has obtained a wide poetical celebrity. Some allegorical interpreters of the poem would have us understand that it is the charms of conversation which have this miraculous power to make men forget their grief. Without at all questioning their efficacy, it may be safely assumed that the poet had in his mind something more material. The drug has been supposed to be opium; but the effects ascribed to the Arabian "haschich"—a preparation of hemp—correspond very closely with those said to be produced by Helen's potion. Sir Henry Halford thought it might more probably be the "hyoscyamus," which he says is still used at Constantinople and in the Morea under the name of "*Nebensch.*" *

Not till the next morning does Telemachus discuss with Menelaus the object of his journey. What little the Spartan king can tell him of the fate of his father is so far reassuring, that there is good hope he is yet alive. But he is—or was—detained in an enchanted island. There the goddess Calypso holds him an unwilling captive, and forces her love upon him. He longs sore for his home in Ithaca; but the spells of the enchantress are too strong. So much has Menelaus learnt, during his own wanderings, while wind-bound

* See Hayman's Odyssey, I. 118, note.

at Pharos in Egypt, from Proteus, "the old man of the sea"—

"Who knows all secret things in ocean pent."

The knowledge had to be forced from him by stratagem. Proteus was in the habit of coming up out of the sea at mid-day to sleep under the shadow of the rocks, with his flock of seals about him. Instructed by his daughter Eidothea—who had taken pity on the wanderers—Menelaus and some of his comrades had disguised themselves in seal-skins* (though much disturbed, as he confesses, by the "very ancient and fish-like smell"), and had seized the ancient sea-god as he lay asleep on the shore. Proteus, like the genie in the Arabian tale, changed himself rapidly into all manner of terrible forms; but Menelaus held him fast until he was obliged to resume his own, when, confessing himself vanquished by the mortal, the god proceeded in recompense to answer his questions as to his own fate, and that of his companion chiefs, the wanderers on their way home from Troy. The transformations of Proteus have much exercised the ingenuity of the allegorists. The pliancy of such principles of interpretation becomes amusingly evident, when one authority explains to us that here are symbolised the wiles

---

* The Esquimaux adopt the very same stratagem in order to get near the seals. "Sir Edward Beecher, in a dissertation on Esquimaux habits read before the British Association, told a story, that he was once levelling his rifle at a supposed seal, when a shipmate's well-known voice from within the hide arrested his aim with the words, 'Don't shoot — it's Husky, sir!'"—Hayman's Odyssey, app. xliii.

of sophistry—another, that it is the inscrutability of truth, ever escaping from the seeker's grasp; while others, again, see in Proteus the versatility of nature, the various ideals of philosophers, or the changes of the atmosphere. From such source had the king learnt the terrible end of his brother Agamemnon, and the ignoble captivity of Ulysses; but for himself, the favourite of heaven, a special exemption has been decreed from the common lot of mortality. It is thus that Proteus reads the fates for the husband of Helen:—

> "Thee to Elysian fields, earth's farthest end,
> Where Rhadamanthus dwells, the gods shall send;
> Where mortals easiest pass the careless hour;
> No lingering winters there, nor snow, nor shower,
> But ocean ever, to refresh mankind,
> Breathes the shrill spirit of the western wind."

The grand lines of Homer are thus grandly rendered by Abraham Moore. Homer repeats the description of the Elysian fields, the abode of the blest, in a subsequent passage of the poem, which has been translated almost word for word—yet as only a poet could translate it—by the Roman Lucretius. Mr Tennyson has the same great original before him when he makes his King Arthur see, in his dying thought,

> "The island-valley of Avilion,
> Where falls not hail nor rain nor any snow,
> Nor ever wind blows loudly; but it lies
> Deep-meadowed, happy, fair with orchard lawns,
> And bowery hollows crowned with summer sea."

The calm sweet music of these lines has charmed

many a reader who never knew that the strain had
held all Greece enchanted two thousand years ago. It
has been scarcely possible to add anything to the quiet
beauty of the original Greek, but the English poet has
at least shown exquisite skill in the setting of the jewel.
But Homer has always been held as common property
by later poets. Milton's classical taste had previously
adopted some of the imagery; the "Spirit" in the
'Masque of Comus' speaks of the happy climes which
are his proper abode : —

> " There eternal summer dwells,
> And west winds, with musky wing,
> About the cedarn alleys fling
> Nard and cassia's balmy smells."

Gladly would Menelaus have kept the son of his old
comrade with him longer as a guest, but Telemachus is
impatient to rejoin his galley, which waits for him at
Pylos. His host reluctantly dismisses him, not without
parting gifts; but the gift which the king would have
had him take—a chariot and yoke of three swift horses
—the island-prince will not accept. Ithaca has no
room for horse-coursing, and he loves his rocky home all
the better.

> " With me no steeds to Ithaca shall sail.
> Such leave I here—thy grace, thy rightful vaunt,
> Lord of a level land, where never fail
> Lotus, and rye, and wheat, and galingale :
> No room hath Ithaca to course, no mead—
> Goat-haunted, dearer than horse-feeding vale."

There is much consternation in the palace of Ulysses
when the absence of Telemachus is at last discovered.

Antinous and his fellow-revellers are struck with astonishment at the bold step he has suddenly taken, and with alarm at the possible result. Antinous will man a vessel at once, and waylay him in the straits on his return. The revelation of this plot to Penelope by Medon, the herald, one of the few faithful retainers of Ulysses' house, makes her for the first time aware of her son's departure; for old Eurycleia has kept her darling's secret safe even from his mother. In an agony of grief she sits down amidst her sympathising maidens, and bewails herself as "twice bereaved," of son and husband. She lifts her prayer to Minerva, and the goddess hears. When Penelope has wept herself to sleep, there stands at the head of her couch what seems the form of her sister Iphthimè, and assures her of her son's safety: he has a guardian about his path "such as many a hero would pray to have." Even in her dream, Penelope is half conscious of the dignity of her visitor; and, true wife that she is, she prays the vision to tell her something of her absent husband. But such revelation, the figure tells her, is no part of its mission, and so vanishes into thin air. The sleeper awakes—it is a dream indeed; but it has left a lightness and elasticity of spirit which the queen accepts as an augury of good to come.

CHAPTER III.

ULYSSES WITH CALYPSO AND THE PHÆACIANS.

The fifth book of the poem opens with a second council of the gods. It has been remarked with some truth that the gods of the Odyssey are, on the whole, more dignified than those of the Iliad. They are divided in this poem, as well as in the other, in their loves and hates towards mortals, but their dissensions are neither so passionate nor so grotesque. Minerva complains bitterly to the Ruler of Olympus of the injustice with which her favourite Ulysses is treated, by being kept so long an exile from his home. She, too, repeats the indignant protest which the poet had before put into the mouth of Mentor, which has found vent in all times and ages, from Job and the Psalmist downwards, when in the bitterness of a wounded spirit men rebel against what seems the inequality of the justice of heaven; that "there is one event to the righteous and the wicked;" nay, that the wicked have even the best of it. "Let never king henceforth do justly and love mercy; but let him rule with iron hand and work all iniquity; for lo! what is Ulysses' reward?" Jupiter is moved by the appeal.

He at once despatches Mercury to the island of Calypso,
to announce to her that Ulysses must be released from her
toils; such is his sovereign will, and it must be obeyed.
The description of the island-grotto in which Calypso
dwells is one of the most beautiful in Homer, and it is
a passage upon which our English translators have de-
lighted to employ their very best powers. Perhaps
Leigh Hunt's version is the most simply beautiful, and
as faithful as any. Mercury has sped on his errand:—

> "And now arriving at the isle, he springs
> Oblique, and landing with subsided wings,
> Walks to the cavern 'mid the tall green rocks,
> Where dwelt the goddess with the lovely locks.
> He paused; and there came on him, as he stood,
> A smell of cedar and of citron wood,
> That threw a perfume all about the isle;
> And she within sat spinning all the while,
> And sang a low sweet song that made him hark and smile.
> A sylvan nook it was, grown round with trees,
> Poplars, and elms, and odorous cypresses,
> In which all birds of ample wing, the owl
> And hawk, had nests, and broad-tongued waterfowl.
> The cave in front was spread with a green vine,
> Whose dark round bunches almost burst with wine;
> And from four springs, running a sprightly race,
> Four fountains clear and crisp refreshed the place;
> While all about a meadowy ground was seen,
> Of violets mingling with the parsley green."

Calypso recognises the messenger, for the immortals,
says the poet, know each other always. Mercury tells
his errand—a bitter one for the nymph to hear, for she
has set her heart upon her mortal lover. Very hard
and envious, she says, is the Olympian tyrant, to
grudge her this harmless fancy. [She must have
thought in her heart, though the poet does not put

it into words for her, that Jupiter should surely have some sympathy for weaknesses of which he set so remarkable an example.] But she will obey, as needs she must. Ulysses shall go; only he must build himself a boat, for there is none in her island. She goes herself to announce to him his coming deliverance. She finds him sitting pensively, as is his wont, on the sea-beach, looking and longing in the direction of Ithaca.

> "Companion of the rocks, the livelong light,
> He dreaming on the shore, but not at rest,
> With groans and tears and lingering undelight
> Gazed on the pulses of the ocean's breast."

His heart is in his native island; but, sooth to say, he makes the best of his present captivity. He endures, if he does not heartily reciprocate, the love of his fair jailer. The correspondence in many points of these Homeric lays with the legends of mediæval Christendom, especially with those of Arthur and his Round Table, has been already noticed. It has been said also that, on the whole, the moral tone of Homer is far purer. But there is one bright creation of mediæval fiction which finds no counterpart in the song of the Greek bard. It was only Christianity—one might almost say it was only mediæval Christianity—which could conceive the pure ideal of the stainless knight who has kept his maiden innocence,—who only can sit in the "siege perilous" and win the holy Grail, "because his heart is pure." Among all the heroes of Iliad or Odyssey there is no Sir Galahad.

Calypso obeys the behest of Jove reluctantly, but

without murmuring. Goddess-like or woman-like, however, she cannot fail to be mortified at the want of any reluctance on her lover's part to leave her. There is something touching in her expostulation:—

> "Child of Laertes, wouldst thou fain depart
> Hence to thine own dear fatherland? Farewell!
> Yet, couldst thou read the sorrow and the smart,
> With me in immortality to dwell
> Thou wouldst rejoice, and love my mansion well.
> Deeply and long thou yearnest for thy wife;
> Yet her in beauty I perchance excel.
> Beseems not one who hath but mortal life
> With forms of deathless mould to challenge a vain strife."

Ulysses' reply is honest and manful:—

> "All this I know and do myself avow.
> Well may Penelope in form and brow
> And stature seem inferior far to thee,
> For she is mortal, and immortal thou.
> Yet even thus 'tis very dear to me
> My long-desired return and ancient home to see.
>
> "But if some god amid the wine-dark flood
> With doom pursue me, and my vessel mar,
> Then will I bear it as a brave man should.
> Not the first time I suffer. Wave and war
> Deep in my life have graven many a scar."

It cannot but be observed, however, that while Penelope's whole thoughts and interests are concentrated upon her absent husband, the longing of Ulysses is rather after his fatherland than his wife. She is only one of the many component parts of the home-scene which is ever before the wanderer's eyes; and not always the most important part, for his aged father and mother and his young son seem to be at least equal

The island on which he has been cast is Scheria,* inhabited by the Phæacians, whose king and people are very far indeed from being of the ordinary type of mortal men. Whether the poet, in his description of these Phæacian islanders, was exercising his imagination only, or indulging his talent for satire, is a controverted question with Homeric critics. Those who would assign this poem of the Odyssey to a different author from the writer or writers of the Iliad, and to a much later date than that commonly given to Homer, have thought that in the good-humoured boastfulness of the Phæacian character, their love of pleasure and novelty, and their attachment to the sea, some Ionian poet was showing up, under fictitious names, the weaknesses of his own countrymen. Others take the Phæacians to be only another name for the Phœnicians, the sailors of all seas, who had probably in their character somewhat of the egotism and exaggeration which have been commonly reputed faults of men who have travelled far and seen much. Whatever may be the true interpretation of the story, or whether there be any interpretation at all, this curious episode in the adventures of Ulysses is unquestionably rather comic than serious. The names are all significant, somewhat after the fashion of those assumed by the Red men. The king (Alcinous) is "Strong-mind," son of "The Swift Seaman," and he has a brother called "Crusher of Men." The nautical names of his courtiers—"Prow-man" and "Stern-man," and the rest— are as palpably conventional as our own Tom Bowline

* Possibly Corfu, if the geography is to be at all identified.

and Captain Crosstree. The hero's introduction to his new hosts presents, nevertheless, one of the most beautiful scenes in the poem. The patriarchal simplicity of the tale cannot fail to remind the reader, as Homer so often does, of the narratives of the earlier Scriptures.

The princess Nausicaa, daughter of the king of the Phæacians, has had a dream. The dream—which comes as naturally to princesses, no doubt, as to other young people—is of marriage; and in this case it could be no possible reproach to the dreamer, since the goddess of wisdom is represented as having herself suggested it. Nor is the dream of any bridegroom in particular, but simply of what seems to us the very prosaic fact that a wedding outfit, which must soon come to be thought of, required household stores of good linen; and that the family stock in the palace, from long disuse, stood much in need of washing. Nausicaa awakes in the morning, and begs of her father to lend her a chariot and a yoke of mules, that she and her maidens may go down to the shore, where the river joins the sea, to perform this domestic duty. The pastoral simplicity of the whole scene is charming. It has all the freshness of those earlier ages when the business of life was so leisurely and jovially conducted, that much of it wore the features of a holiday. The princess and her maidens plunge the linen in the stream, and stamp it clean with their pretty bare feet (a process which will remind an English reader of Arlette and Robert of Normandy, and which may be seen in operation still at many a burn-side in Scotland), and then go

themselves to bathe. An outdoor banquet forms part
of the day's enjoyment; for the good queen, Nausicaa's
mother, has stored the wain with delicate viands and a
goat-skin of sweet wine. When this is over, the girls
begin to play at ball. Ulysses, be it remembered, is
all this while lying fast asleep under his heap of leaves,
and, as it happens, close by the spot where this merry
party are disporting themselves. By chance Nausicaa,
too eager in her game, throws the ball out into the sea;
whereupon the whole chorus of handmaidens raise a cry
of dismay, which at once awakens the sleeper. He is
puzzled, when he comes to himself, to make out where
he is; and still more confounded, when he peers out from
his hiding-place, to find himself in the close neighbourhood of this bevy of joyous damsels, especially when he
bethinks himself of the very primitive style of his present costume; for the scarf which the sea-nymph gave
him as a talisman he had cast into the sea upon his landing, as she had especially charged him. But Ulysses
is far too old a traveller to allow an over-punctilious
modesty to stand in his way when he is in danger of
starving. He has no idea of missing this opportunity
of supplying his wants merely because he has lost his
wardrobe. He extemporises some very slight covering
out of an olive-bough, and, in this strange attire, makes
his sudden appearance before the party. Nausicaa's
maidens all scream and take to flight—very excusably;
but the king's daughter, with a true nobility, stands firm.
She sees only a shipwrecked man, and "to the pure
all things are pure." Ulysses is a courtier as well as a
traveller, and knows much of "cities and men;" and

it is not the flattery of a suppliant, but the quick discernment of a man of the world, which makes him at once assign her true rank to the fair stranger who stands before him. He remains at a respectful distance, while, in the language of Eastern compliment, he compares her to the young palm-tree for grace and beauty, and invokes the blessing of the gods upon her marriage-hour, if she will take pity on his miserable case. Nausicaa recalls her fugitive attendants, and rebukes them for their folly, reminding them that "the stranger and the poor are the messengers of the gods." The shipwrecked hero is supplied at once with food and drink and raiment; and when he reappears, after having bathed and clothed himself, it is with a mien and stature more majestic than his wont, with the "hyacinthine locks" of immortal youth flowing round his stately shoulders —such grace does his guardian goddess bestow upon him, that he may find favour in the sight of the Phæacian princess. She looks upon him now with simple and undisguised admiration, confessing aside to her handmaidens that, when her time for marriage *does* come, she should wish for just such a husband as this godlike stranger. There is nothing unmaidenly in such language from the lips of Nausicaa. To remain unmarried was a reproach in her day, whatever it may be in ours, and a reproach not likely to fall upon a king's daughter; so, looking upon the marriage state as inevitable, and at her age very near at hand, she thinks and speaks of it unreservedly to her companions. Our modern conventional silence on such topics arises in great degree from the fact that a perpetual maidenhood is the inevitable lot of far too many in our over-civilised society, and, being inevitable, is no reproach. It does not consort, therefore, with maidenly dignity to express any interest about marriage, for which an opportunity may never be offered.

But Nausicaa is at least as careful to observe the proprieties, according to her own view of them, as any modern young lady. She will promise the shipwrecked stranger a welcome at her father's court; but he must by no means ride home in the wain with her, or even be seen entering the city in her company. So Ulysses runs by the side of her mules, and waits in a sacred grove near the city gates, until the princess and her party have re-entered the palace. When they have disappeared, he issues forth, and meets a girl carrying a pitcher. It is once more his guardian goddess in disguise. She veils him in a mist, so that he passes the streets unquestioned by the natives (who have no love for strangers), and stands at last in the presence of King Alcinous.

The king of the Phæacians, as well as his queen, boast to be descended from Neptune. His subjects therefore, are, as has been said, emphatically a sea-going people. Ulysses has already seen with admiration, as he passed,

> "The smooth wide havens, and the glorious fleet,
> Wherewith those mariners the great deep tire."

Their galleys, moreover, are unlike any barks that ever walked the seas except in a poet's imagination. King Alcinous himself describes them:—

> "For unto us no pilots appertain,
> Rudder nor helm which other barks obey.
> These, ruled by reason, their own course essay
> Sharing men's mind. Cities and climes they know,
> And through the deep sea-gorges cleaving way,
> Wrapt in an ambient vapour, to and fro
> Sail in a fearless scorn of scathe or overthrow."

The wondrous art of navigation might well seem nothing less than miraculous in an age when all the forces of nature were personified as gods. So, when the great ship Argo carried out her crew of ancient heroes on what was the first voyage of discovery, the fable ran that in her prow was set a beam cut from the oak of Dodona, which had the gift of speech, and gave the voyagers oracles in their distress. Our English Spenser must have had these Phæacian ships in mind when he describes the "gondelay" which bears the enchantress Phædria :—

> "Eftsoone her shallow ship away did slide,
> More swift than swallow sheres the liquid sky,
> Withouten oar or pilot it to guide,
> Or winged canvass with the wind to fly;
> Only she turned a pin, and by-and-by
> It cut a way upon the yielding wave,
> (Ne cared she her course for to apply)
> For it was taught the way which she would have,
> And both from rocks and flats itself could wisely save."

As the men of Phæacia excel all others in seamanship, so also do the women in the feminine accomplishments of weaving and embroidery. But they are not, as they freely confess, a nation of warriors: they love the feast and the dance and the song, and care little for what other men call glory. The palace of Alcinous and its environs are all in accordance with this luxurious type of character. All round the palace lie gardens and orchards, which rejoice in an enchanted climate, under whose influence their luscious products ripen in an unfailing succession :—

> "There in full prime the orchard-trees grow tall,
>   Sweet fig, pomegranate, apple fruited fair,
>   Pear and the healthful olive. Each and all
>   Both summer droughts and chills of winter spare;
>   All the year round they flourish. Some the air
>   Of Zephyr warms to life, some doth mature.
>   Apple grows old on apple, pear on pear,
>   Fig follows fig, vintage doth vintage lure;
> Thus the rich revolution doth for aye endure."

When the traveller enters within the palace itself, he finds himself surrounded with equal wonders.

> "For, like the sun's fire or the moon's, a light
>   Far streaming through the high-roofed house did pass
>   From the long basement to the topmost height.
>   There on each side ran walls of flaming brass,
>   Zoned on the summit with a blue bright mass
>   Of cornice; and the doors were framed of gold;
>   Where, underneath, the brazen floor doth glass
>   Silver pilasters, which with grace uphold
> Lintel of silver framed; the ring was burnished gold.

> "And dogs on each side of the doors there stand,
>   Silver and gold, the which in ancient day
>   Hephæstus wrought with cunning brain and hand,
>   And set for sentinels to hold the way.
>   Death cannot tame them, nor the years decay.
>   And from the shining threshold thrones were set,
>   Skirting the walls in lustrous long array,
>   On to the far room, where the women met,
> With many a rich robe strewn and woven coverlet.

"There the Phæacian chieftains eat and drink,
While golden youths on pedestals upbear
Each in his outstretched hand a lighted link,
Which nightly on the royal feast doth flare.
And in the house are fifty handmaids fair;
Some in the mill the yellow corn grind small;
Some ply the looms, and shuttles twirl, which there
Flash like the quivering leaves of aspen tall;
And from the close-spun weft the trickling oil will fall."

King Alcinous sits on his golden throne, "quaffing his wine like a god." His queen, Arete, sits beside him, weaving yarn of the royal purple. Warned by his kind friend the princess, Ulysses passes by the king's seat, and falls at the feet of the queen. In the court of Phæacia—whether the story be disguised fact or pure fiction, whether the poet was satiric or serious—the ruling influence lies with the women. The mist in which Minerva had enveloped his person melts away; and while all gaze in astonishment at his sudden appearance, he claims hospitality as a shipwrecked wanderer, and then, after the fashion of suppliants, seats himself on the hearth-stone. The hospitality of Alcinous is prompt and magnificent. He bids one of his sons rise up and cede the place of honour to the stranger. If he be mortal man, the boon he asks shall be granted : but it may be that he is one of the immortals, who, as he gravely assures his guest, often condescend to come down and share the banquets of the Phæacians, and make themselves known to them face to face. Ulysses assures his royal host, in a passage which is in itself sufficient to mark the subdued comedy of the episode, that far from having any claim to divinity, he is very mortal indeed, and wholly taken up at present with one of the most inglorious of mortal cravings :—

> " Nothing more shameless is than Appetite,
> Who still, whatever anguish load our breast,
> Makes us remember, in our own despite,
> Both food and drink. Thus I, thrice wretched wight,
> Carry of inward grief surpassing store,
> Yet she constrains me with superior might,
> Wipes clean away the memory-written score,
> And takes whate'er I give, and taking, craveth more." *

There is every appliance to satisfy appetite, however, in the luxurious halls of Alcinous. While Ulysses is seated at table, Queen Arete, careful housewife as she is with all her royalty, marks with some curiosity that the raiment which their strange guest wears must have come from her own household stores—so well does she know the work of herself and her handmaidens. This leads to a confession on Ulysses' part of his previous interview with Nausicaa, whom he praises, as he had good right to do, as wise beyond her years. So charmed is the king with his guest's taste and discernment, that he at once declares that nothing would

---

* This humorous impersonation of one of the lowest, but certainly the strongest, influences of our common nature, has been made use of by later writers. The Roman poets Virgil and Persius take up Homer's idea; and Rabelais, closely following the latter, introduces his readers to a certain powerful personage whom he found surrounded by worshippers—" one Master Gaster, the greatest Master of Arts in the world." [" Gaster " is Homer's Greek word, which Mr Worsley renders by " appetite," but which is more literally Englished by the old Scriptural word " belly."]

please him better than to retain him at his court in the character of a son-in-law. Ulysses (whose fate it is throughout his wanderings to make himself only too interesting to the fair sex generally) is by this time too much accustomed to such proposals to show any embarrassment. With his usual diplomacy he puts the question aside—bowing his acknowledgments only, it may be, though Homer does not tell us even so much as this. The one point to which he addresses himself is the king's promise to send him safe home, which he accepts with thankfulness. Before they retire for the night, the queen herself does not disdain to give special orders for their guest's accommodation. She bids her maidens prepare

> "A couch beneath the echoing corridor,
> And thereon spread the crimson carpets fair,
> Then the wide coverlets of richness rare,
> And to arrange the blankets warm and white,
> Wherein who sleepeth straight forgets his care.
> They then, each holding in her hand a light,
> From the great hall pass forth, and spread the robes aright."

The combination of magnificence with simplicity is of a wholly Oriental character. The appliances of the court might be those of a modern Eastern potentate; yet the queen is a thrifty housekeeper, the princess-royal superintends the family wash, and the five sons of the royal family, when their sister comes home, themselves come forward and unyoke her mules from the wain which has brought home the linen.

The next day is devoted to feasting and games in honour of the stranger. Amongst the company sits the blind minstrel Demodocus, in whose person it has been thought that the poet describes himself—

> "Whom the Muse loved, and gave him good and ill;
> Ill, that of light she did his eyes deprive,
> Good, that sweet minstrelsies divine at will
> She lent him, and a voice men's ears to thrill.
> For him Pontonous silver-studded chair
> Set with the feasters, leaning it with skill
> Against the column, and with tender care
> Made the blind fingers feel the harp suspended there."

Such honour has the bard in all lands. The king's son does not disdain to guide "the blind fingers;" and when the song is over, the herald leads him carefully to his place at the banquet, where his portion is of the choicest — "the chine of the white-tusked boar." The subject of his lay is the tale which charms all hearers—Phæacian, Greek, or Roman, ancient or modern, then as now—the tale of Troy. Touched with the remembrances which the song awakens, Ulysses wraps his face in his mantle to hide his rising tears. The king marks his guest's emotion: too courteous to allude to it, he contents himself with rising at once from the banquet-table, and giving order for the sports to begin. Foot-race, wrestling, quoit-throwing, and boxing, all have their turn; and in all the king's sons take their part, not unsuccessfully. It is suggested at last that the stranger, who stands silently looking on, should exhibit some feat of strength or skill. Ulysses declines—he has no heart just now for pastimes. Then one of the young Phæacians, Euryalus, who has just won the wrestling-match, gives vent to an ungracious taunt. Their guest, he says, is plainly no hero, nor versed in the noble science of athletics; he must be some skipper of a merchantman, "whose talk is all of cargoes." He brings down upon himself a grand rebuke from Ulysses:—

> "Man, thou hast not said well; a fool thou art.
> Not all fair gifts to all doth God divide,
> Eloquence, beauty, and a noble heart.
> One seems in mien poor, but his feebler part
> God crowns with language, that men learn to love
> The form, so feelingly the sweet words dart
> Within them. First in councils he doth prove,
> And, 'mid the crowd observant, like a god doth move.

> "Another, though in mould of form and face
> Like the immortal gods he seems to be,
> Hath no wise word to crown the outward grace
> So is thine aspect fair exceedingly,
> Wherein no blemish even a god might see;
> Yet is thine understanding wholly vain."

Then the hero who has thrown the mighty Ajax in the wrestling-ring, who is swifter of foot than any Greek except Achilles, and who has been awarded that matchless hero's arms as the prize of valour against all competitors,—rises in his wrath, and gives his gay entertainers a taste of his quality. Not deigning even to throw off his mantle, he seizes a huge stone quoit, and hurls it, after a single swing, far beyond the point reached by any of the late competitors. The astonished islanders crouch to the ground as it sings through the air above their heads. Once roused, Ulysses launches out into the self-assertion which has been remarked as being common to all the heroes of Homeric story. He challenges the whole circle of bystanders to engage with him in whatsoever contest they will—

> "All feats I know that are beneath the sun."

He will not, indeed, compare himself with some of the heroes of old, such as were Hercules and Eurytus;

> "But of all else I swear that I stand first,
> Such men as now upon the earth eat bread."

None of the Phæacians will accept the challenge. The king commends the spirit in which the stranger has repelled the insult of Euryalus, and with the gay good-humour which marks the Phæacian character, confesses that in feats of strength his nation can claim no real excellence, but only in speed of foot and in seamanship; or, above all, in the dance—in this no men can surpass them. His guest shall see and judge. Nine grave elders, by the king's command (and here the satire is evident, even if we have lost the application) stand forth as masters of the ceremonies, and clear the lists for dancing. A band of selected youths perform an elaborate ballet, while the minstrel Demodocus sings to his harp a sportive lay, not over-delicate, of the stolen loves of Mars and Venus, and their capture in the cunning net of Vulcan. If it must be granted that this song forms a strong exception to the purity of Homer's muse, it has also been fairly pleaded for him, that it is introduced as characteristic of an unwarlike nation and an effeminate society. But even in his lightest mood the poet has no sort of sympathy with a wife's unfaithfulness. He takes his gods and goddesses as he found them in the popular creed; bad enough, and far worse than the mortal men and women of his own poetical creation. But his own morals are far higher than those of Olympus. Even in this questionable ballad of the Phæacian minstrel the point of the jest is in strong contrast to some of the comedies of a more modern school. It is on the detected culprits, not on the injured husband, that the ridicule of gods and men is mercilessly showered. When the ballet is concluded, two of the king's sons, at their father's bidding, perform a sort of minuet, in which ball-play is introduced. Ulysses expresses his admiration of the whole performance in words which sound like solemn irony :—

> "O king, pre-eminent in word and deed,
> Of late thy lips the threatening vaunt did make
> That these thy dancers all the world exceed—
> Now have I seen fulfilment of thy rede;
> Yea, wonder holds me while I gaze thereon."

So all passes off with pleasant compliments between hosts and guest. The king and his twelve peers present Ulysses with costly gifts, and Euryalus, in pledge of regret for his late unseemly speech, offers his own silver-hilted sword with its ivory scabbard.

From the games they pass again to the banquet; and one more glimpse is given us of the gentle Nausicaa, perfectly in keeping with the maiden guilelessness of her character. Ulysses—still radiant with the more than human beauty which the goddess has bestowed upon him—moves to his place in the hall.

> "He from the bath, cleansed from the dust of toil,
> Passed to the drinkers; and Nausicaa there
> Stood, moulded by the gods exceeding fair.
> She on the roof-tree pillar leaning, heard
> Odysseus; turning, she beheld him near.
> Deep in her breast admiring wonder stirred,
> And in a low sweet voice she spake this wingèd word.
>
> "'Hail, stranger-guest! when fatherland and wife
> Thou shalt revisit, then remember me,
> Since to me first thou owest the price of life.'
> And to the royal virgin answered he:
> 'Child of a generous sire, if willed it be
> By Thunderer Zeus, who all dominion hath,
> That I my home and dear return yet see,
> There at thy shrine will I devote my breath,
> There worship thee, dear maid, my saviour from dark death.'"

It is not easy to discover, with any certainty, what the Greek poet meant us to understand as to the feelings of Nausicaa towards Ulysses. It has been said that Love, in the complex modern acceptation of the term, is unknown to the Greek poets. Nor is there, in this passage, any approach to the expression of such a feeling on the part of the princess. Yet, had the scene found place in the work of a modern poet, we should have understood at once that, without any kind of reproach to the perfect maidenly delicacy of Nausicaa, it was meant to show us the dawn of a tender sentiment—nothing more—towards the stranger-guest whom the gods had endowed with such majestic graces of person, who stood so high above all rivals in feats of strength and skill, whose misfortunes surrounded him with a double interest, and, above all, in whom she felt a kind of personal property as his deliverer.

The Greek historian Plutarch chivalrously defends the young princess from the charge of forwardness, which ungallant critics brought against her as early as his day. It was no marvel, he says, that she knew and valued a hero when she saw him, and preferred him to the carpet-knights of her own country, who were good only at the dance and the banquet. But with her it was, after all, a sentiment, and no more; but which might have ripened into love, under other circumstances, had the hero of her maiden fancy been as free to choose as she was.

So vanishes from the page one of the sweetest creations of Greek fiction—the more charming to us, as coming nearest, perhaps, of all to the modern type of feeling. The farewell to Nausicaa is briefly said; and Ulysses, sitting by King Alcinous at the banquet, pays a high compliment to the blind minstrel, and gives him a new theme for song. Since he knows so well the story of the great Siege, let him now take his lyre, and sing to them of the wondrous Horse. Demodocus obeys. He sings how the Greeks, hopeless of taking Troy by force of arms, had recourse at last to stratagem: how they constructed a huge framework in the shape of a horse, ostensibly an offering to the gods, and then set fire to their sea-camp, and sailed away—for home, to all appearance—leaving an armed company hidden in the womb of the wooden monster; how the Trojans, after much doubt, dragged it inside their walls, and how, in the night-time, the Greeks issued from their strange ambush, and spread fire and sword through the devoted city. And all along Ulysses is the hero of the lay. He is the leader of the venturous band who thus carried their lives in their hands into the midst of their enemies: he it is who, "like unto Mars," storms the house of Deiphobus, who had taken Helen to wife after the death of his brother Paris, and restores the Spartan princess to her rightful lord. Tears of emotion again fill the listener's eyes; and again the courteous king bids the minstrel cease, when he sees that some chord of mournful remembrance is struck in the heart of his guest. But he now implores him, as he has good right to do, to tell them who he really is. Why does the Tale of Troy so move him? The answer, replies the stranger, will be a long tale, and sad to tell; but his very name, he proudly says, is a history—"I am Ulysses, son of Laertes!"

CHAPTER IV.

ULYSSES TELLS HIS STORY TO ALCINOUS.

THE narrative, which Ulysses proceeds to relate to his host, takes back his story to the departure of the Greek fleet from Troy. First, on his homeward course, he and his comrades had landed on the coast of Thrace, and laid waste the town of the Ciconians. Instead of putting to sea again with their plunder, the crews stayed to feast on the captured beeves and the red wine. "Wrapt in the morning mist," large bodies of the natives surprised them at this disadvantage, and they had to re-embark with considerable loss. This was the beginning of their troubles. They were rounding the southern point of Greece, when a storm bore them out far to sea, and not until sunset on the tenth day did they reach an unknown shore—the land of the Lotus-eaters—

> "Who, on the green earth couched beside the main,
> Seemed ever with sweet food their lips to entertain."

To determine the geography of the place is as difficult as to ascertain the natural history of the lotus, though critics have been very confident in doing both.* The effect of the seductive food on the companions of Ulysses is thus described :—

> "And whoso tasted of their flowery meat
> Cared not with tidings to return, but clave
> Fast to that tribe, for ever fain to eat,
> Reckless of home-return, the tender Lotus sweet."

Those who ate of it had to be dragged back by main force to their galleys, and bound fast with thongs, so loath were they to leave that shore of peaceful rest and forgetfulness. In the words of our own poet, who has founded one of the most imaginative of his poems on this incident of Ulysses' voyage, so briefly told by Homer—

> "Most weary seemed the sea, weary the oar,
> Weary the wandering fields of barren foam.
> Then some one said—'We will return no more:'
> And all at once they sang—'Our island-home
> Is far beyond the wave; we will no longer roam.'" †

---

* The Greek historian Herodotus places a tribe of lotus-eaters, "who live by eating nothing but the fruit of the lotus," on the coast of Africa, somewhere near Tripoli. Pliny and other ancient writers on natural history speak of this fruit as in shape like an olive, with a flavour like that of figs or dates, not only pleasant to eat fresh, but which, when dry, was made into a kind of meal. The English travellers Shaw and Park found (in the close neighbourhood of Herodotus' lotus-eaters) what they thought to be the true lotus—a shrub bearing "small farinaceous berries, of a yellow colour and delicious taste." Park says—"An army may very well have been fed with the bread I have tasted made of the meal of the fruit, as is said by Pliny to have been done in Libya." There is also a water-plant in Egypt mentioned by Herodotus under the name of lotus—probably the *Nymphæa lotus* of Linnæus.

† Tennyson, "The Lotus-Eaters."

It has been thought that here we have possibly the bread-fruit tree of the South Sea Islands, with some hint of the effect produced by their soft and enervating climate, and that the voyage of Ulysses anticipated in some degree the discoveries of Anson and Cook. It is curious that, in Cook's case, the seductions of those islands gave him the same trouble as they did Ulysses; for several of his crew thought, like the Greek sailors, that they had found an earthly paradise for which they determined to forget home and country, and had to be brought back to their ship by force. But the lotus-land of the poet is an ideal shore, to which some of us moderns may have travelled as well as Ulysses. Its deepest recesses will have been reached by the Buddhist who attains his coveted state of perfect beatitude, the "Nirvâna," in which a man has found out that all having and being, and more especially doing, are a mistake. It is the *dolce far niente* of the Italian; the region free from all cares and responsibilities—"beyond the domain of conscience"—which Charles Lamb, half in jest and half in earnest, sighed for.

Bearing away from the shore of the Lotus-eaters, Ulysses and his crew next reached the island where the Cyclops dwell—a gigantic tribe of rude shepherds, monsters in form, having but one eye planted in the centre of their foreheads, who know neither laws, nor arts, nor commerce. Adventure and discovery have always a charm for Ulysses; and it was with no other motive, as he pretty plainly confesses, that he landed with his own ship's crew to explore these unknown regions. The present adventure had a horrible conclusion for some of his companions. Alone, in a vast cave near the shore, dwelt the giant Polyphemus, a son of Neptune the sea-god, and folded his flocks in its deep recesses. They did not find the monster within: but the pails of brimming milk, and huge piles of cheese, stood ranged in order round the walls of the cavern. Nothing would satisfy Ulysses but to await the owner's return. At evening he came, driving his flocks before him; and, as was his wont, began to busy himself in his dairy operations. By the red glow of the firelight he soon discovered the intruders, as they crouched in a corner. In vain they made appeal to his hospitality, reminding him that strangers were under the special care of Jupiter. What care the Cyclops race for the gods? So he seized two of the unhappy Greeks, dashed them on the ground—"like puppies"—devoured them, blood, bones, and all, after the manner of giants, and washed down his horrible supper with huge bowls of milk. Two more furnished him with breakfast in the morning. But the craft of Ulysses was more than a match for the savage. He had carried with him on his dangerous expedition (having a kind of presentiment that it would prove useful) a skin of wine of rare quality and potency, and of this he gave Polyphemus to drink after his last cannibal meal. Charmed with the delicious draught, the giant begged to know his benefactor's name. The answer of Ulysses is the oldest specimen on record of the art of punning.

" 'Hear then; my name is Noman. From of old
My father, mother, these my comrades bold,

> Give me this title.' So I spake, and he
> Answered at once with mind of ruthless mould:
> 'This shall fit largess unto Noman be—
> Last, after all thy peers, I promise to eat thee."

Then, overcome by the potent drink, the savage lay down to sleep. Ulysses had prepared the thin end of a huge club of olive-wood, and this, pointed and well hardened in the fire, he and his comrades thrust into his single eye-ball, boring it deep in, "as the shipwright doth an auger." Roaring with pain, and now fairly sobered, Polyphemus awoke, and shouted for help to his brother-Cyclops who dwelt in the neighbouring valleys. They came; but to all their questions as to what was the matter, or who had injured him, he only answered "*Noman!*"—and his friends turned away in disgust. After groping vainly round the cave in search of his tormentors, Polyphemus rolled the huge stone from the mouth of his den, and let his sheep go out, feeling among them for his captives, who would probably try thus to escape. But again the wit of the Ithacan chief proved too subtle for his enemy. The great sheep had been cunningly linked together three abreast, and every middle sheep carried a Greek tied under his belly; Ulysses, after tying the last of his companions, clinging fast to the wool of a huge ram, the king of the flock. So did they all escape to rejoin their anxious comrades. But when all had embarked, and rowed to a safe distance, then Ulysses stood high upon his deck, and shouted a taunting defiance to his enemy. The answer of Polyphemus was a huge rock hurled with all his might towards the voice, which fell just short of the vessel. Again Ulysses shouted, and bade him tell those who should hereafter ask him who did the deed, that it was even Ulysses the Ithacan. The Cyclops groaned with rage and grief—an ancient oracle had forewarned him of the name; but will the great Ulysses please to return, that he may entertain such a hero handsomely? He would have shown himself more simple than his enemy if he had. Then the blind monster lifted his cry to his great father the Sea-god, and implored his vengeance on his destroyer.

The one-eyed giant of Homer's story became a very popular comic character in classical fiction. The only specimen of the old Greek satyric drama, as it was called—a peculiar kind of comedy, in which satyrs were largely introduced—is a play by Euripides, 'The Cyclops,' in which the principal incident is the blinding of Polyphemus by Ulysses. The monster rushes out of his cave, with his eye-socket burnt and bleeding, and stretches his arms across the entrance to intercept the escape of Ulysses, who creeps out between his legs. He roars out with pain, and is taunted by the "Chorus,"—a party of satyrs whom he has made his slaves, and who now rejoice in their deliverance.

"*Chorus.* Why make this bawling, Cyclops?
  Cyclops.   I am lost!
  Ch. Thou'rt dirty, anyhow.
  Cyc.   Yea, and wretched too!
  Ch. What! hast got drunk, and fallen into the fire?
  Cyc. Noman hath slain me!
  Ch.   Then thou'rt wronged by no man.
  Cyc. Noman hath blinded me!

Ch.   Then thou'rt not blind.
Cyc. Would ye were so!—
Ch.   Why, how could *no man* blind thee?
Cyc. Ye mock me.—Where is Noman?
Ch.   Nowhere, Cyclops.
Cyc. O friends, if ye would know the truth, yon wretch
    Hath been my ruin—gave me drink, and drowned me!
Ch. Ay—wine is strong, we know, and hard to deal with.

The poet Theocritus, in one of his Idylls, gives us Polyphemus, before his blindness, in love with the beautiful nymph Galatæa, who, having another lover with two eyes in the young shepherd Acis, does not encourage the addresses of the Cyclops. This is part of his remonstrance:—

> " I know, sweet maiden, why thou art so coy;
> Shaggy and huge, a single eyebrow spans
> From ear to ear my forehead, whence one eye
> Gleams, and an o'er-broad nostril o'er my lip.
> Yet I—this monster—feed a thousand sheep,
> That yield me sweetest draughts at milking-tide.
>
> . . . . . .
>
> But thou mislik'st my hair?—Well, oaken logs
> Are here, and embers yet a-glow with fire;
> Burn, if thou wilt, my heart out, and my eye—
> My lonely eye, wherein is my delight."
>   —Theocritus, Idyll xi. (Calverley's transl.)

This love-story of the Cyclops is better known, perhaps, to English readers, through Handel's Pastoral, 'Acis and Galatæa.'

The imprecation of Polyphemus was heard, and Ulysses was long to suffer the penalty of his bold deed. Yet, but for the weakness of his comrades, he might perhaps have escaped it. For, as they sailed on over unknown seas, they won the friendship of the King of the Winds. He feasted them a whole month on his brass-bound island; and he, too, like all the world of gods and men, asked eagerly for the last news of the heroes of Troy. So charmed was Æolus with his guest, that on his departure he presented Ulysses with an ox-hide tied with a silver cord, in which all the winds were safely confined, save only Zephyr, who was left loose to waft the voyagers safely home. So for nine days and nights they ran straight for Ithaca, Ulysses himself at the helm, for he would trust it to no other hand. And now they had come in sight of the rocks of their beloved island—so near that they could see the smoke go up from the herdsmen's camp-fires; when, overcome with long watching, the chief fell asleep upon the deck. Then the greed and curiosity of his companions tempted them to examine the ox-hide bag. It must be some rich treasure, surely, thus carefully tied up and stowed away. They opened it; out rushed the imprisoned blasts, and drove them back in miserable plight to the island of Æolus,—much to that monarch's astonishment. In vain did Ulysses tell his unlucky story, and beg further help from the ruler of the storms; Æolus would have nothing more to do with such an ill-starred wretch, upon whom there rested so manifestly the curse of heaven, but drove him and his companions out to sea again with ignominy.

A second time the voyagers fell into the hands of cannibals. They moored their ships in the harbour of the Læstrygonians,—in the description of which there has been lately traced a strong likeness to the bay of Balaclava—

> "A rock-surrounded bay,
> Whence fronting headlands at the mouth outrun,
> Leaving a little narrow entrance-way,
> Wherethrough they drive the vessels one by one."

These Læstrygonians were a giant race, like the Cyclops, and of an equally barbarous character. One of the exploring party, whom Ulysses sent to reconnoitre, they seized and devoured on the spot, and then hurled rocks down on the ships as they lay moored in the land-locked harbour, and speared the unfortunate crews, "like fish," as they swam from the wrecks. Ulysses only had moored outside, and escaped with his single ship by cutting his cable.

Pursuing his sad voyage, he had reached the island of Ææa, where dwelt the enchantress Circe "of the bright hair," daughter of the Sun. Here he divided his small remaining force into two bands, one of which, under his lieutenant, Eurylochus, explored the interior of the island, while Ulysses and the rest kept guard by their ship. Hidden deep in the woods, they came upon the palace of Circe.

> "Wolves of the mountain all around the way,
> And lions, softened by the spells divine,
> As each her philters had partaken, lay.
> These cluster round the men's advancing line
> Fawning like dogs, who, when their lord doth dine,
> Wait till he issues from the banquet-hall,
> And for the choice gifts which his hands assign
> Fawn, for he ne'er forgets them—so these all
> Fawn on our friends, whom much the unwonted sights appal.

> "Soon at her vestibule they pause, and hear
> A voice of singing from a lovely place,
> Where Circe weaves her great web year by year,
> So shining, slender, and instinct with grace
> As weave the daughters of immortal race."

The abode of Circe presents quite a different picture from the grotto of Calypso.* There, all the beauties were those of nature in her untouched luxuriance; here we have all the splendour of an Oriental interior, enriched with elaborate art—wide halls of polished marble, silver-studded couches, and vessels of gold.

Throwing wide the shining doors, the enchantress gaily bade them enter; and all, save only the more prudent Eurylochus, accepted the invitation. They drank of her drugged cup; then she struck them with her wand, and lo! they became swine in form, yet retaining their human senses. Eurylochus, after long watching in vain for the reappearance of his comrades, returned alone with his strange tale to his chief, who at once set forth to the rescue. On his way through the forest, he was suddenly accosted by a fair youth, bearing a wand of gold — none other than the god Mercury—who gave him a root of wondrous virtue—

---

* So sensible was Fénélon of this contrast that, in his romance already mentioned, when he describes Calypso's cave, he thinks it necessary, like a true Frenchman of the days of the great Louis, almost to apologise for the rude simplicity of nature, as hardly befitting so enchanting a personage. There were no statues, he says, no pictures, no painted ceilings, but the roof was set with shells and pebbles, and the want of tapestry was supplied by the tendrils of a vine.

> "Black, with a milk-white flower, in heavenly tongue
> Called Moly."*

Armed with this, he can defy all Circe's enchantments. She mixed for him the same draught, struck him with her wand, and bid him "go herd with his companions;" but potion and spell had lost their power. Circe had found her master, and knew it could be no other than "the many-wiled Ulysses," of whose visit she had been forewarned. Not even the magic virtues of the herb Moly, however, enable him to resist her proffered love; and Ulysses, by his own confession, forgot Penelope in the halls of Circe, as afterwards in the island of Calypso. It may be offered as his apology, that it was absolutely necessary for him to make himself agreeable to his hostess, in order to obtain from her (as he does at once) the deliverance of his companions from her toils; but this does not explain his sending for the rest of his crew from the ship, and spending a whole year in her society. The ingenious critics who insist on shaping a moral allegory

---

* So the Spirit, in Milton's "Comus," gives to the brother of the Lady a sure antidote to the spell of the enchanter (himself represented as a son of Circe):—

> "Among the rest a small unsightly root,
> But of divine effect, he culled me out;
> The leaf was darkish, and had prickles on't,
> But in another country, as he said,
> Bore a bright golden flower, but not in this soil:
> Unknown, and like esteemed, and the dull swain
> Treads on it daily with his clouted shoon;
> And yet more med'cinal is it than that Moly
> That Hermes once to wise Ulysses gave."

out of the story of the Odyssey confess to having found a stumbling-block in this point of the narrative. It sounds very plausible to say that in Circe is personified sensual pleasure; that those who partake of her cup, and are turned into swine, are those who brutalise themselves by such indulgences; that the herb Moly—black at the root, but white and beautiful in the blossom—symbolises "instruction" or "temperance," by which the temptations of sense are to be resisted. But Ulysses' victory over the enchantress, and his subsequent relations to her, fall in but awkwardly with any moral of any kind. To say that Ulysses knows how to indulge his appetites with moderation, and therefore escapes the penalties of excess—that he is the master of Pleasure, while his companions become its slaves—is to make the parable teach a very questionable form of morality indeed, since it represents self-indulgence as praiseworthy, if we can only manage to escape the consequences.

But it was not until Ulysses had been reminded by his companions that he was forgetting his fatherland, that he besought his fair entertainer to let him go. Reluctantly she consented, bound by her oath—warning him, as they parted, that toil and peril lay before him, and that if he would learn his future fate, he must visit the Regions of the Dead, and there consult the shade of the great prophet Tiresias.

Ulysses goes on to describe to the king of the Phæacians his voyage on from the island of Ææa, under the favouring gales which Circe sends him:—

> "All the day long the silvery foam we clave,
>   Wind in the well-stretched canvas following free,
>   Till the sun stooped beneath the western wave.
>   And darkness veiled the spaces of the sea.
>   Then to the limitary land came we
>   Of the sea-river, streaming deep, where dwell,
>   Shrouded in mist and gloom continually,
>   That people, from sweet light secluded well,
> The dark Cimmerian tribe, who skirt the realms of hell."

Who these Cimmerians were is not easily discoverable. Their name was held by the Greeks a synonym for all that was dark and barbarous in the mists of antiquity. It appears, nevertheless, in the earlier historians as the appellation of a real people; some rash ethnologists, tempted chiefly by the similarity of name, have tried to identify them with the Cymry—the early settlers of Wales. The Welsh are notoriously proud of their ancient origin, but it is doubtful how far they would accept the poet's description of their ancestral darkness, or the neighbourhood to which he here assigns them.

CHAPTER V.

THE TALE CONTINUED—THE VISIT TO THE SHADES.

THE eleventh book of the poem, in which Ulysses goes down to the Shades to consult the Dead, has been considered by some good authorities as a later interpolation into the tale. The solemn grandeur of the whole episode is remarked as out of character with the light and easy narrative into which it has been woven. Be this as it may, the passage has a strong interest in itself. It is the solitary glimpse which we have of the poet's creed as to the state of disembodied spirits. It is at least not in contradiction to the views which are disclosed—scantily enough—by the author of the Iliad, though here we find them considerably more developed. It is a gloomy picture at the best; and we almost cease to wonder at the shrinking from death which is so often displayed by the Homeric heroes, when we find their future state represented as something almost worse, to an active mind, than annihilation.

> " Never the Sun that giveth light to men
>   Looks down upon them with his golden eye,

> Or when he climbs the starry arch, or when
> Slope toward the earth he wheels adown the sky;
> But sad night weighs upon them wearily."

They reached the spot, says Ulysses, described to him at parting by Circe, where the dark rivers Acheron and Cocytus mix at the entrance into Hades. The incantations which she had carefully enjoined were duly made; a black ram and ewe were offered to the powers of darkness, and their blood poured into the trench which he had dug—"a cubit every way."

> " Forthwith from Erebus a phantom crowd
> Loomed forth, the shadowy people of the dead,—
> Old men, with load of earthly anguish bowed,
> Brides in their bloom cut off, and youths unwed,
> Virgins whose tender eyelids then first shed
> True sorrow, men with gory arms renowned,
> Pierced by the sharp sword on the death-plain red.
> All these flock darkling with a hideous sound,
> Lured by the scent of blood, the open trench around."

But he had been charged by Circe not to allow the ghastly crew to slake their thirst, until he had evoked the shade of Tiresias, the blind prophet of Thebes, who retained his art and his honours even in these regions of the dead. So he kept them off with his sword,—not suffering even the phantom of his dead mother Anticleia, who came among the rest, to taste, until the great prophet appeared, leaning on his golden staff.

> " To the bloody brink
> He stooped, and with his shadowy lips made shrink
> The sacrificial pool that darkling lay
> Beneath him."

From the lips of Tiresias Ulysses has learnt the future which awaits him. On the coast of Sicily he should find pasturing the herds and flocks of the Sun: if he and his comrades left them uninjured, they should soon see again their native Ithaca; if they laid sacrilegious hands on them, he alone should escape, and reach home after long suffering.

The shade of his mother has been sitting meanwhile in gloomy silence, eyeing the coveted blood. Not until she had drank of it might she open her lips to speak, or have power to recognise her son. To his eager inquiries as to her own fate and that of his father Laertes she made answer that she herself had died of grief, and that the old man was wearing out a joyless life in bitter anxiety.

> "Therewith she ended, and a deep unrest
> Urged me to clasp the spirit of the dead,
> And fold a phantom to my yearning breast.
> Thrice I essayed, with eager hands out-spread
> Thrice like a shadow or a dream she fled,
> And my hands closed on unsubstantial air."

As they talked together, there swept forth out of the gloom a crowd of female shapes—the mothers of the mighty men of old. There came Tyro, beloved by the sea-god Neptune, from whom sprang Neleus, father of Nestor: next followed Antiope, who bore to Jupiter Amphion and Zethus, who built the seven-gated Thebes; Iphimedeia, mother of the giants Otus and Ephialtes, who strove to take heaven itself by storm; Alcmena, Leda, Ariadne, and a crowd of the heroines of Greek romance, who had found the loves of the gods more or less disastrous in their earthly lot, and who were reaping, in the gloomy immortality which the poet assigns them, such consolation as they might from knowing themselves the mothers of heroes.

Here Ulysses would have ended his tale, and for a while a charmed silence falls upon his Phæacian audience. But the king would hear more. Did he see, in the realms of the dead, no one of those renowned champions who had fought with him at Troy?

Yes—if his host cares to listen, Ulysses can tell him a sad tale of some of his old comrades. He saw the great Agamemnon there, and heard from his lips the treachery of the adulterous Clytemnestra. Antilochus and Patroclus, too, he had recognised, and Ajax; but the latter, retaining in the world below the animosities of earthly life, had stood far aloof, and sullenly refused to speak a word in answer to his successful rival. The only one who reveals anything of the secrets of his prison-house is Achilles. He asks of his adventurous visitor what has prompted him to risk this intrusion into the gloomy dwelling, where the dead live indeed, but without thought or purpose, mere shadows of what they were. And when Ulysses attempts to comfort him with the thought of the deathless glory which surrounds his name, the hopelessness of his answer sets forth, in the darkest colours, that gloomy view of human destiny which breaks out from time to time in the creed of the poet, and which belongs to the character of his favourite hero. Whether the Odyssey did or did not come from the same hand as the Iliad, at least Achilles is the same in both. In the former poem we find him indulging in all the mournful irony of the Hebrew Preacher, in his perplexed thought before he was led to "the conclusion of the whole matter"—complaining, like him, that "one event happeneth to all," and that "the wise man dieth as the fool;" that he, the bravest and most beautiful of living heroes, would have to meet the same lot as his victim Lycaon; so here, in the Odyssey, he adopts the text that "a living dog is better than a dead lion:"—

> "Rather would I, in the sun's warmth divine,
> Serve some poor churl who drags his days in grief,
> Than the whole lordship of the dead were mine."

Such was the immortality to which Paganism condemned even its best and bravest.

One touching inquiry both Agamemnon and Achilles put to their visitor from the upper world. How fare their sons? Where is Orestes?—asks the great king. Did Neoptolemus, in the later days of the war, prove himself worthy of his father?—inquires Achilles. When he has been assured of this, the shade of the mighty hero, well satisfied,

> "Passed striding through the fields of asphodel."

There is no distinct principle of reward or punishment discernible in the regions of the dead, as seen by Ulysses. Indeed, anything like happiness in this shadowy future seems incompatible with the feelings put into the mouth of Achilles. Orion, the mighty hunter, appears to enjoy something like the Red Indian's paradise—pursuing, in those shadowy fields, the phantoms of the wild creatures which he slew on earth; but, with this exception, there is no hint of pleasurable interest or occupation for the mighty dead. Punishments there are for notorious offenders against the majesty of the gods:—

> "There also Tantalus in anguish stood,
> Plunged in the stream of a translucent lake;
> And to his chin welled ever the cold flood.
> But when he rushed, in fierce desire to' break
> His torment, not one drop could he partake.
> For as the old man stooping seems to meet
> That water with his fiery lips, and slake
> The frenzy of wild thirst, around his feet,
> Leaving the dark earth dry, the shuddering waves retreat.

> "Also the thick-leaved arches overhead
> Fruit of all savour in profusion flung,
> And in his clasp rich clusters seemed to shed.
> There citrons waved, with shining fruitage hung,
> Pears and pomegranates, olive ever young,
> And the sweet-mellowing fig: but whensoe'er
> The old man, fain to cool his burning tongue,
> Clutched with his fingers at the branches fair,
> Came a strong wind and whirled them skyward through the air."

> "And I saw Sisyphus in travail strong
> Shove with both hands a mighty sphere of stone:
> With feet and sinewy wrists he, labouring long,
> Just pushed the vast globe up, with many a groan;
> But when he thought the huge mass to have thrown
> Clean o'er the summit, the enormous weight
> Back to the nether plain rolled tumbling down.
> He, straining, the great toil resumed, while sweat
> Bathed each laborious limb, and his brow smoked with heat."

Both these are examples of punishment inflicted in the Shades below, not for an evil life, but for personal offences against the sovereign of the gods. Tantalus had been admitted as a guest to the banquet of the immortals, and had stolen their nectar and ambrosia to give to his fellow-men. Sisyphus had been, it is true, a notorious robber on earth, but the penalty assigned him was for the higher crime of betraying an amour of Jupiter's which had come to his knowledge. The stone of Sisyphus has been commonly taken as an illustration of labour spent in vain; but a modern English poet has found in it a beautiful illustration of the indestructibility of hope. In one of Lord Lytton's 'Tales of Miletus,' when Orpheus visits the Shades in search of his lost wife—

> "He heard, tho' in the midst of Erebus,
> Song sweet as his Muse-mother made his own;
> It broke forth from a solitary ghost,
> Who, up a vaporous hill,
>
> "Heaved a huge stone that came rebounding back,
> And still the ghost upheaved it and still sang.
> In the brief pause from toil while towards the height
> Reluctant rolled the stone,
>
> "The Thracian asked in wonder, 'Who art thou,
> Voiced like Heaven's lark amidst the night of Hell?'
> 'My name on earth was Sisyphus,' replied
> The phantom. 'In the Shades
>
> "I keep mine earthly wit; I have duped the Three.[*]
> They gave me work for torture; work is joy.
> Slaves work in chains, and to the clank they sing.'
> Said Orpheus, 'Slaves still hope!'
>
> "'And could I strain to heave up the huge stone
> Did I not hope that it would reach the height?
> There penance ends, and dawn Elysian fields.'
> 'But if it never reach?'"

---

[*] The judges of the Dead—Minos, Rhadamanthus, and Æacus.

> "The Thracian sighed, as looming through the mist
> The stone came whirling back. 'Fool,' said the ghost,
> 'Then mine, at worst, is everlasting hope.'
> Again uprose the stone."

Ulysses confesses that he did not see all he might have seen; for, when the pale ghosts in their ten thousands crowded round him with wild cries, the hero lost courage, fled back to his ship, and bade his comrades loose their cables, and put out at once to sea.

They passed the island where the twin sisters, the Sirens, lay couched in flowers, luring all passing mariners to their destruction by the fascination of their song. Forewarned by Circe, the chief had stopped the ears of all his crew with melted wax, and had made them bind him to the mast, giving them strict charge on no account to release him, however he might entreat or threaten—for he himself, true to his passion for adventure, would fain listen to these dangerous enchantresses. So, as they drifted close along the shore, the Sirens lifted their voices and sang as follows—every word of Mr Worsley's translation is Homer's, except the single phrase in brackets:—

> "Hither, Odysseus, great Achaian name,
> Turn thy swift keel, and listen to our lay;
> Since never pilgrim to these regions came
> In black ship [on the azure waves astray],
> But heard our sweet voice ere he sailed away,
> And in his joy passed on, with ampler mind.
> We know what labours were in ancient day
> Wrought in wide Troia, as the gods assigned;
> We know from land to land all toils of all mankind."

But the deaf crew rowed on, and not until the sound of

the strain had died away in the distance did they unbind their captain, in spite of his angry protests. They pass the strait that divides Sicily from Italy, where on either hand lurked the monsters Scylla and Charybdis—impersonations, it may be, of rocks and whirlpools—but which they escaped, with the loss of six out of the crew, by help of Circe's warnings and directions. But that our own Spenser's 'Faery Queen' is perhaps even less known to the majority of English readers than the Odyssey of Homer (by grace of popular translations), it might be needless to remind them how the whole of Sir Guyon's voyage on the "Idle Lake" is nothing more or less than a reproduction of this portion of Ulysses' adventures.* The five mermaidens, who entrap unwary travellers with their melody, address the knight as he floats by in a strain which is the echo of the Sirens'—

> " O thou fayre son of gentle Fäery,
> That art in mightie arms most magnifyde
> Above all knights that ever batteill tryde,
> O turn thy rudder hitherwarde awhile :
> Here may thy storme-bett vessell safely ryde :
> This is the port of rest from troublous toyle,
> The worldes sweet Inn from pain and wearisome turmoyle."

The enchantress Acrasia, with her transformed lovers —the " seeming beasts who are men in deed "—is but a copy from Circe ; while the " Gulf of Greediness " yawning on one side of the Lake—

> "That deep engorgeth all this worldës prey "—

and on the other side the " Rock of Vile Reproach,"

* 'Faery Queen,' Book ii. c. 12.

whose fatal magnetic power draws in all who try to shun the whirlpool opposite, are the Scylla and Charybdis of Homer.

At length the voyagers reached the shore where the oxen of the Sun were pastured. In vain did Ulysses, remembering the prophecy of Tiresias, bid them steer on and leave the land unvisited. Eurylochus, his lieutenant, broke out at last into something like mutiny. He had some show of reason, when he complained of his chief, almost in the words of Sir Dinadan to Sir Tristram in the 'Morte d'Arthur,' that he was tired of such mad company, and would no longer follow a man to whose iron frame the toils and dangers which wore out ordinary mortals were a mere disport. Seeing that the rest backed Eurylochus in his proposal to land and rest, Ulysses was fain to give way, after exacting a vow that at least none of them should lay sacrilegious hands upon the sacred herds, since they had store of corn and wine, the parting gifts of Circe, on board their vessel. But stress of weather detained them in the anchorage a whole month, until corn and wine were exhausted, and they had to snare birds and catch fish—a kind of food which a Greek seaman especially despised—to keep them from starving. Then at last, while their chief had withdrawn to a quiet spot, and fallen asleep wearied with long prayer, Eurylochus persuaded the rest to break their vow, and slay the choicest of the oxen. Terrible prodigies followed the unhallowed meal; the skins of the slain animals moved and crawled after their slayers, and the meat, while roasting on the spits, uttered fearful cries and groans. One of the old allegorical interpreters has drawn from this incident a moral which, however fanciful, is not without a certain beauty and appositeness of illustration—the sins of the wicked, he says, dog their steps, and cry aloud against them. When next they put to sea, Jupiter raised winds and waves to punish them; for the Sun had threatened that, if such insult went unavenged, he would light the heavens no more, but go down and shine in Hades. Their ship was riven by a thunderbolt, and Ulysses alone, sole survivor of all his crew, after once more narrowly escaping the whirlpool of Charybdis, after floating nine days upon the broken mast, was cast ashore on the island of Calypso, and there detained until his release by the intercession of Minerva, as has been told, which had ended in this second shipwreck on the coast of his present entertainers.

CHAPTER VI.

ULYSSES' RETURN TO ITHACA.

THE hero, at his departure, is loaded with rich presents of honour from his Phæacian hosts. The twelve princes of the kingdom each contribute their offering—gold and changes of raiment; the king adds a gold drinking-cup of his own, and Queen Arete a mantle and tunic. The careful queen also supplies him with a magnificent chest, in which she packs his treasures with her own royal hands; and Ulysses secures the whole with a "seaman's knot," whose complications will defy the uninitiated—a secret which he has learnt from Circe, and which he seems to have handed down to modern sailors. Thus equipped, he is sent on board one of the magic galleys, to be conveyed home to his native Ithaca. They embark in the evening, and early the next morning the crew—apparently in order to give the adventure the half-ludicrous turn which seems inseparable from the Phæacians—land their passenger, still sound asleep, and leave him on shore under an olive-tree, with his store of presents heaped beside him. When he awakes, he fails to recognise his native island, for Minerva has spread a mist over it. The goddess herself presently accosts him, in the form of a shepherd, and listens patiently to a story which the hero invents, with his usual readiness, to account for his presence on the island. Then she discovers herself, with a somewhat ironical compliment on the inveterate craftiness which has led him to attempt to impose on the wisest of the immortals. She tells him news of his wife and of his son, and promises him her help against the accursed suitors. She lays her golden wand upon him, and lo! the majestic presence which had touched the maiden fancy of Nausicaa, and won him favour in the eyes of the Phæacian court (to say nothing of Circe and Calypso) has at once given place to the decrepitude of age. The ruddy cheeks grow wrinkled, the bright eyes are dimmed, the flowing locks turned grey, and Ulysses is, to all appearance, an aged beggar, clad in squalid rags. Thus disguised, so that none shall recognise him till his hour comes, he seeks shelter, by direction of the goddess, with his own swineherd Eumæus.

Eumæus is one of the most characteristic personages in the poem, and has given the most trouble to the poet's various critics. He occupies a sort of forester's lodge in the woods, where the vast herds of swine belonging to the absent king are fed by day, and carefully lodged at night. Though he is but a keeper of swine, Homer applies to him continually the epithets "godlike," and "chief of men," which he commonly uses only of territorial lords such as Ulysses and Menelaus. He not only has subordinates in his employ, but an attendant slave, whom he has purchased with his own money; and he so far exercises an independent right of property in the animals which are under his care as to kill and dress them—two at a time, such is the lavish hospitality of the age—to feast the stranger-guest who has now come to him. It may be straining a point to see in him, as one of the most genial of Homeric critics does, "a genuine country gentleman of the age of Homer;" but his position, so far as it is possible to compare it with anything at all in modern social life, appears something like that of the agricultural steward of a large landed proprietor, with whom his relations, though strictly subordinate, are of a highly confidential and friendly character. The charge of the swine would be a much more important office in an age when, as is plain from many passages both in the Iliad and the Odyssey, the flesh of those animals held a place of honour at the banquets of chiefs and kings: and as we find that even the sons of a royal household did not think the keeping of sheep beneath their dignity, so the care of other animals would by no means imply a menial position. Eumæus, indeed, turns out to be himself of princely birth—stolen in his childhood by a treacherous nurse from the island where his father was king, sold by Phœnician merchants to Laertes in Ithaca, and brought up in his household almost as a son, and regarding the lost Ulysses "as an elder brother." Very loyal is he to the house of his benefactors; prefacing his meal by a prayer that his lord may yet return in safety, and grieving specially that the lady Penelope, in her present troubles, has seldom the opportunity to see or speak with him in the kindly intercourse of old. The cordial and simple relations between master and servant—even though the servant was commonly nothing more or less than a purchased slave—are a striking feature, very pleasant to dwell upon, in these Homeric poems. They remind us, as Homer does so often, of similar pictures in the sacred narrative of the gentler affections which redeemed so often the curse of slavery—of the little captive Israelite maiden whose concern for her Syrian master led to his cure, and of the faithful steward, "born in the house" of Abraham, whom the childless patriarch once thought to make his heir.

Eumæus entertains the stranger right hospitably—warning him, at the same time, not to pretend, as others have often done in the hope of reward, to bring tidings of the lost Ulysses. His guest's own story he will be glad to hear. The hero is always ready at narrative, whether the tale is to be fact or fiction. At present he chooses fiction; he gives his listener an imaginary history of his past life, as a Cretan chief who had seen much good service in many lands, especially under King Idomeneus at Troy, but who had met with a succession of disasters since. Of course he had seen and known Ulysses; had heard of him since the fall of Troy; and he offers his host a wager that he will yet return. Eumæus will hear nothing of such flattering hopes; by this time his men are coming in from the field, and when the swine are safely housed, supper and bedtime follow. But the night is bitter cold, and Ulysses has nothing but his beggar's rags. He indirectly begs a covering from his host by an ingenious story, very characteristic of the style of the lighter episodes of the Odyssey. He relates an adventure of his own while lying in ambush, one winter night, under the walls of Troy. Dr Maginn's translation of this passage, in the old English ballad style, though somewhat free, preserves fairly the spirit and humour of the original :—

" Oh ! were I as young and as fresh and as strong
As when under Troy, brother soldiers among,
In ambush as captains were chosen to lie
Odysseus and King Menelaus and I!

" They called me as third, and I came at the word,
And reached the high walls that the citadel gird;
When under the town we in armour lay down
By a brake in the marshes with weeds overgrown.
The night came on sharp, bleak the north wind did blow,
And frostily cold fell a thick shower of snow.

" Soon with icicles hoar every shield was frozen o'er ;
But they who their cloaks and their body-clothes wore
The night lightly passed, secure from the blast,
Asleep with their shields o'er their broad shoulders cast;
But I, like a fool, had my cloak left behind,
Not expecting to shake in so piercing a wind.

" My buckler and zone—nothing more—had I on ;
But when the third part of the night-watch was gone,
And the stars left the sky, with my elbow then I
Touched Odysseus, and spoke to him, lying close by—
' Noble son of Laertes, Odysseus the wise,
I fear that alive I shall never arise.

" ' In this night so severe but one doublet I wear—
Deceived by a god—and my cloak is not here,
And no way I see from destruction to flee.'
But soon to relieve me a project had he.
In combat or council still prompt was his head,
And into my ear thus low whisp'ring he said :—

"'Let none of the band this your need understand;
Keep silent.' Then, resting his head on his hand,—
'Friends and comrades of mine,' he exclaimed, 'as a sign,
While I slept has come o'er me a dream all divine.
It has warned me how far from the vessels we lie,
And that some one should go for fresh force to apply;

"'And his footsteps should lead, disclosing our need,
To King Agamemnon, our chieftain, with speed.'
Thoas rose as he spoke, flung off his red cloak,
And running, his way with the message he took;
While, wrapt in his garment, I pleasantly lay
Till the rise of the golden-throned queen of the day.

"'If I now were as young, and as fresh, and as strong,
Perhaps here in the stables you swine-herds among
Some a mantle would lend, as the act of a friend,
Or from the respect that on worth should attend;
But small is the honour, I find, that is paid
To one who, like me, is so meanly arrayed.'"

—(Maginn's 'Homeric Ballads.')

The self-laudation which the hero, speaking in another person, takes the opportunity to introduce, is in perfect keeping with his character throughout.

The hint so broadly given is quite successful, and Eumæus provides his guest with some warm coverings and a place near the fire; but he himself will not sleep so far from his charge. Wrapped in a mighty windproof cloak, he takes up his quarters for the night under the shelter of a rock, hard by the lair of his swine.

CHAPTER VII.

THE RETURN OF TELEMACHUS FROM SPARTA.

THE story returns to Telemachus, whom we left at Sparta. His stay at that court has been prolonged a whole month, for which the excuse, we must suppose, is to be found in the hospitalities of Menelaus and the fascinations of Helen. No wonder that his guardian goddess admonishes him in a dream that, under his present circumstances, such delays are dangerous. Penelope has a hard time of it in his absence, even her father pressing her to marry some one of her suitors. Nay, Minerva more than hints—though we beg our readers not to accept such an insinuation against Penelope, even on the authority of a goddess—that Eurymachus, one of the richest of the rivals, is beginning to find favour in her eyes. Telemachus is roused once more to action : awakening his young friend Pisistratus, he proposes that they should set out on their return at once—before the day breaks. The son of the old "Horse-tamer" sensibly reminds him that driving in the dark is very undesirable, and it is agreed to wait for the morning. Menelaus, with genuine courtesy, refrains from any attempt to detain his guests longer than seems agreeable to themselves. A portion of his speech, as rendered by Pope, has passed into a popular maxim as to the true limits of hospitality, and has been quoted, no doubt, by many, with very little idea that they were indebted to Homer for the precept—

> " True friendship's laws are by this rule exprest—
> Welcome the coming, speed the parting guest."

Another maxim of the hospitable Spartan has long been adopted by Englishmen—that all wise men, who have a long day's journey before them, should lay in a substantial breakfast. This the travellers do, and then prepare to mount their chariot; Telemachus bearing with him, as the parting gift of his royal host, a bowl of silver wondrously chased, "the work of Vulcan"— too fair to come from any mortal hand—which Menelaus had himself received from the King of Sidon; while Helen adds an embroidered robe "that glistened like a star," one of many which she has woven with her own hands, which she begs him to keep to adorn his bride on her marriage-day. Even as they part, lo! there is an omen in the sky—an eagle bearing off a white goose in her talons. Who shall expound it? Menelaus, who is appealed to, is no soothsayer. Helen alone can unlock the riddle :—

> " Just as this eagle came from far away,
> Reared in the bleak rock, nursling of the hill,
> And in the stormy ravin of his wild will
> Seized on the white goose, delicately bred,—
> So brave Ulysses, after countless ill,
> Comes from afar off, dealing vengeance dread."

Telemachus blesses her for the happy interpretation, and promises that, should the word come true, he will worship the fair prophetess in Ithaca as nothing less than a divinity. Whether or no he made good his vow the poet does not tell us. Worse mortals have been canonised both in ancient and modern calendars. And whether Helen was honoured thus in Ithaca or not, she certainly was at Sparta, where we are told that she displayed her new powers as a divinity once at least in a very appropriate manner—transforming a child of remarkable ugliness, at the prayer of its nurse, into a no less remarkable beauty.

The young men make their first evening halt at Pheræ, as before, and reach Nestor's court at Pylos next day. Telemachus insists on driving straight to the bay where his patient crew still await him with the galley —for he knows old Nestor will try to detain him, out of kindness, if he once set foot again in the palace— and instantly on his arrival they hoist sail for home. They round the peninsula in the night, and with the morning's dawn they sight the spiry peaks of Ithaca. The crew moor the vessel in a sheltered bay, while Telemachus—to escape the ambuscade which he knows to have been laid for him—makes straight for the swineherd's lodge, instead of entering the town. As he draws near the threshold, the watch-dogs know his step, and run out to greet him ; Eumæus himself, in his delight at the meeting, drops from his hands the bowl of wine which he was carefully mixing as a morning draught for his disguised guest, and falls on his young lord's neck, kissing him, and weeping tears of joy.

" Thou, O Telemachus, my life, my light,
  Returnest; yet my soul did often say
  That never, never more should I have sight
  Of thy sweet face, since thou didst sail away.
  Enter, dear child, and let my heart allay
  Its yearnings; newly art thou come from far:
  Thou comest all too seldom—fain to stay
  In the thronged city, where the suitors are,
Silently looking on while foes thy substance mar."

Ulysses preserves his disguise, and rises from his seat to offer it to the young chief. But Telemachus, like all Homer's heroes, is emphatically a gentleman; and he will not take an old man's place, though that man be but a poor wayfarer clad in rags. When he has broken his fast at his retainer's table, he would know from him who the stranger is. Eumæus repeats the fictitious history which he has heard from Ulysses, and Telemachus promises the shipwrecked wanderer relief and protection. He sends Eumæus to announce his own safe return to Penelope; and when the father and son are left alone, suddenly Minerva appears—visible only to Ulysses and to the dogs, who cower and whine at the supernatural presence—and bids him discover himself to his son. The beggar's rags fall off, a royal robe takes their place, and he resumes all the majesty of presence which he had worn before. But Telemachus does not recognise the father whom he has never known; the sudden transformation rather suggests to him some heavenly visitant. He was but an infant when Ulysses went to Troy; and even when his father assures him of his identity, he will not believe. There is a quiet sadness, but no reproach, in the hero's reply :—

> "Other Odysseus cometh none save me.
> Behold me as I am! By earth and sea
> Scourged with affliction, in the twentieth year,
> Safe to mine own land at the last I flee."

It is long before either, in their first emotion, can find words to tell their story. Ulysses takes his son fully into his counsels, and charges him to keep the news of his return as yet a secret even from his mother, until they two shall discover who among the household can be trusted to aid them in the extermination of the intruders and their powerful retinue. He knows that his day of vengeance is come at last, and nothing less than this will satisfy him. Telemachus has some timorous misgivings, according to his nature—What are they two against so many? But Ulysses knows that the gods are on his side—Minerva and the Father of the gods himself; or shall we say with the allegorists, in this case, the Counsels of Heaven and the Justice of Heaven? There is a grand irony in the question which he puts to his son—"Thinkest thou these allies will suffice, or shall we seek for other helpers?"

CHAPTER VIII.

ULYSSES REVISITS HIS PALACE.

GREAT is the consternation amongst the riotous crew in the palace, when they find that Telemachus has escaped their toils, and has returned; and great the joy of Penelope when she hears this good news from Eumæus, which yet she hardly believes, until it is confirmed by a visit from her son in person. The suitors receive him with feigned courtesy, though some among them have already determined on his assassination. The swineherd follows to the palace, bringing with him, by command of Telemachus, the seeming beggar—for Ulysses has undergone a second transformation, and is once more an aged man in mean apparel. As a poor wanderer, dependent on public charity, he is sure to find that ready admittance into the royal precincts which is so necessary for carrying out his plans of vengeance, without raising the suspicions of the present occupants. On the way they are met by Melanthius the goatherd, whose character stands in marked contrast to that of Eumæus. He is utterly faithless to his absent master's interests, and has become the ready instrument of his enemies. With mocking insolence he jeers at Eumæus and his humble acquaintance, and even goes so far as to spurn the latter with his foot. Ulysses fully justifies his character for patience and endurance; though for a moment he does debate in his heart the alternative, whether he should break the skull of the scoffer with his club, or lift him from his feet and dash his brains out on the ground. As he draws near the gates of his own palace he espies another old retainer, of a different type, belonging to a race noted in all lands and ages for its fidelity. There lies on the dunghill, dying of old age, disease, and neglect, his dog Argus—the companion of many a long chase in happier days. The dog has all Eumæus's loyalty, and more than his discernment. His instinct at once detects his old master, even through the disguise lent by the goddess of wisdom. Before he sees him, he knows his voice and step, and raises his ears—

> " And when he marked Odysseus in the way,
> And could no longer to his lord come near,
> Fawned with his tail, and drooped in feeble play
> His ears. Odysseus turning wiped a tear."

Eustathius (who made none the worse archbishop because he was a thorough lover of Homer) has remarked, somewhat pertinently, that the fate of his dog draws from the imperturbable Ulysses the tears which he never sheds for any thought of Penelope. But such lesser pathetic incidents have often, in actual life, a stronger emotional effect than is produced by the deeper affections.* But he masters his emotion, for this is no time to betray himself, and follows Eumæus through the entrance-doors. It is poor Argus's last effort, and the old hound turns and dies—

> "Just having seen Odysseus in the twentieth year."

The story is told by the Greek poet with somewhat more prolixity of detail than suits our modern notions of the pathetic, but the pathos of the incident itself is of the simplest and purest kind.

In beggar's guise Ulysses enters his own hall, and makes his rounds of the party who sit there at table, soliciting some contribution of broken meat to his wallet. None is so hard of heart as to refuse, except Antinous. In vain does Ulysses compliment him on his princely beauty, and remind him of the uncertainty of fortune, as evidenced by his own present case:—

> "Once to me also sorrow came not near,
> And I had riches and a noble name,
> And to the wandering poor still gave, whoever came."

> "Legions of slaves and many thousand things
> I held, which God doth on the great bestow—
> All that the ownership of large wealth brings.
> But Zeus the Thunderer, for he willed it so,
> Emptied my power, and sent a wave of woe."

Antinous haughtily bids him stand off, and when Ulysses expresses his wonder that in so fair a body

---

* When Adam Bede speaks roughly to his mother, and then tenderly to his dog Gyp, the author thus moralises on his inconsistency: "We are apt to be kinder to the brutes that love us than to the women that love us. Is it because the brutes are *dumb?*"

should dwell so mean a spirit, hurls a stool at him. The blow does not shake the strong frame of Ulysses, who moves to the doorway, lays down his wallet, and lifts his voice in solemn imprecation to the Powers on high who protect the stranger and the poor :—

> "Hear me, ye suitors of the queen divine!
> Men grieve not for the wounds they take in fight,
> Defending their own wealth, white sheep or kine;
> But me (bear witness!) doth Antinous smite
> Only because I suffer hunger's bite,
> Fount to mankind of evils evermore.
> Now may Antinous, ere his nuptial night,
> If there be gods and furies of the poor,
> Die unavenged, unwept, upon the palace-floor."

Even some amongst the young man's companions are horrified by this reckless violation of the recognised laws of charity and hospitality. One of them speaks out in strong rebuke :—

> "Not to thine honour hast thou now let fall,
> Antinous, on the wandering poor this blow.
> Haply a god from heaven is in our hall,
> And thou art ripe for ruin: I bid thee know,
> Gods in the garb of strangers to and fro
> Wander the cities, and men's ways discern;
> Yea, through the wide earth in all shapes they go,
> Changed, yet the same, and with their own eyes learn
> How live the sacred laws—who hold them, and who spurn."

This is one of those noble passages in which the creed of the poet soars far above his mythology. The god who is the avenger of broken oaths, and the protector of the poor and the stranger, though he bears the name of Zeus or Jupiter, is a power of very different type from the Ruler of Olympus, who indulges his sensual passions in base amours with mortals,—who in the Iliad is perpetually engaged in domestic wrangles with his queen, and even in the Odyssey wreaks a weak vengeance on Ulysses merely to gratify the spite of Neptune.

> "Meanwhile Telemachus sat far apart,
> Feeding on fire; and deeper and more drear
> Grew the sharp pang, that he saw stricken there
> His own dear father, and the flower of kings.
> Yet from his eyelids he let fall no tear,
> But, filled in soul with dark imaginings,
> Silently waved his head, and brooded evil things."

Additional insults await the hero in his own hall. There comes from the town a sturdy beggar, known as Irus—"the messenger"—by a kind of parody on the name of the rainbow goddess, Iris, who performs the same office for the immortals. Jealous of a rival mendicant, such as Ulysses appears, he threatens to drive him from the hall. Ulysses quietly warns him to keep his hands off—there is room enough for both. The young nobles shout with delight at a quarrel which promises such good sport, and at once form a ring for the combatants, and undertake to see fair play. When the disguised king strips off his squalid rags for the boxing-match, and discovers the brawny chest and shoulders for which he was remarkable, Irus trembles at the thought of encountering him. But it is too late: with a single blow Ulysses breaks his jaw, and drags him out into the courtyard. The revellers now hail the conqueror with loud applause, and award him the prize of victory—a goat-paunch filled with mince-meat and blood, the prototype, apparently, both of the Scotch haggis and the English black-pudding. Amphinomus—who has already shown something of a nobler nature than the rest—adds a few words of generous sympathy: he sees in the wandering mendicant one who has known better days, and pledges him in a cup of wine, with a hope that brighter fortunes are yet in store. Ulysses is touched with pity for the fate which the young man's evil companions are inevitably drawing on him. He had heard, he tells him, of his father, Nisus—had known him, doubtless, in fact—a wise and good man; such ought the son to be. He adds a voice of ominous warning, tinged with that saddened view of man at his best estate which continually breaks forth, even amidst the lighter passages of the poet.

> "Earth than a man no poorer feebler thing
> Rears, of all creatures that here breathe or move;
> Who, while the gods lend health, and his knees string,
> Boasts that no sorrow he is born to prove.
> But when the gods assail him from above,
> Then doth he bear it with a bitter mind,
> Dies without help, or liveth against love."

Penelope now descends from her chamber for a moment into the hall, to have speech with her son. The goddess Minerva has shed on her such radiant grace and beauty, that her appearance draws forth passionate admiration from Eurymachus. She does but taunt him in reply: most suitors, she says, at least bring presents in their hand; these of hers do but rob, where others give freely. They are all stung sufficiently by her words to produce at once from their stores some costly offerings—embroidered robes, chains and brooches and necklaces of gold and electrum. The queen, after the practical fashion of the age, is not too disdainful to carry them off to her chamber; while Ulysses—as indeed seems more in accordance with his character—secretly rejoices to see his wife thus "spoiling the Egyptians." Some commentators have apologised for this seeming meanness on the part of Penelope by the explanation, that she does it to inspire them with false hopes of her choosing one of them now at last for her husband, and so lulling them into a false security in order to insure their easier destruction. But it is best to take the moral tone of these early poems honestly, as we find it, and not attempt to force it into too close agreement with our own.

After some further acts of insult, still borne with a wrathful endurance by Ulysses, the company quit the hall, as usual, for the night. Then Penelope descends again from her chamber, and sitting by the hearth, bids a chair be set also for the wandering stranger: she will hear his tale. He represents himself to her as the brother of King Idomeneus of Crete, and as having once in his brother's absence entertained the great Ulysses in his halls. To Penelope's eager questions, by which she seeks to test his veracity, he answers by describing not so much the person of her husband as his distinctive dress. The queen recognises, in this description, the curiously-embroidered mantle which she had worked for him, and the golden clasp, "linked with twin stars," which she had fastened with her own hands when he parted from her to go to Troy. She breaks into floods of tears at the recollection; while the disguised Ulysses sets his eyes hard, "as though they were of horn or steel," and checks his rising tears. He comforts her with the assurance that he brings recent news of her hero—of his shipwreck and visit to the Phæacians; that he is even now on his way to Ithaca, last heard of in the neighbouring island of Dulichium, within easy reach of home; nay, this very year, he would be content to pledge himself, Ulysses shall stand once more in his own halls. Incredulous, yet thankful for the comfort, the queen orders the wanderer to be taken to the bath, and entertained as an honoured guest. But he refuses all attendance save that of the aged Eurycleia. She marks with wonder his likeness to her absent master; but such resemblance, he assures her, has been noticed frequently by others. As she bathes his feet, her eyes fall on a well-remembered scar, left by a wound received from a boar's tusk in his youth while hunting on Mount Parnassus with his grandsire Autolycus.*

* From this maternal ancestor Ulysses might have inherited a large share of the subtlety which distinguished him. Autolycus was the reputed son of Hermes (Mercury)—the god of thieves —and did not in that point disgrace his blood. He was said to have the power of so transforming all stolen property, that the owner could not possibly recognise it. Shakespeare borrows the name, and some of the qualities, for one of his characters in the 'Winter's Tale'—"Autolycus, a rogue," as he stands in the list of *dramatis personæ*, who professes himself "not naturally honest, but sometimes so by chance."

The old nurse doubts no longer. She lets the foot fall heavily, and upsets the bath.

> " Surely thou art Ulysses—yes, thou art—
> My darling child, and I not knew my king
> Till I had handled thee in every part !"

He puts his hand upon her throat, and forcibly checks her outcry; his purpose is not to be known openly as yet, for he feels there are few, even of his own household, whom he can trust. He charges her —even on pain of death, much as he loves her—to keep his secret; then, refusing all softer accommodation, he lies down in the vestibule on a couch of bullhide, not sleeping, but nursing his wrath in a fever of wakefulness.

CHAPTER IX.

THE DAY OF RETRIBUTION.

THE morrow is a festival of Apollo. It is kept by the riotous crew in the halls of Ulysses with more than their usual revelry. The disguised hero himself, feeding at a small table apart by command of Telemachus, is still subject to their insults. But portents are not wanting of their impending doom. In the midst of the feast Minerva casts them into fits of ghastly laughter; the meat which they are eating drips with gore; and the seer Theoclymenus—a refugee under the protection of Telemachus—who has been of late their unwilling companion, sees each man's head enveloped in a misty darkness, and the whole court and vestibule thronged with ghostly shapes. He cries out in affright, and tells them what sight he sees; but they only answer him with mockery, and threaten to drive him forth as one who has lost his wits. After warning them of the fate which he foresees awaiting them, he quits the company. They turn upon Telemachus, and taunt him with his sorry choice of guests: first yon lazy disreputable vagabond, and now this prating would-be soothsayer. The young man makes no reply, but watches his father anxiously; and Ulysses still bides his time.

The queen meanwhile has bethought her of a new device, to put off yet awhile the evil day in which she must at length make her choice amongst her importunate lovers. She unlocks an inner chamber where the treasures of the house are stored, and draws from its case Ulysses' bow, the gift of his dead friend Iphitus, which he had not taken with him to Troy. Before she carries it down, she lays it fondly on her knees, and weeps as she thinks of its absent master. One cunning feat she remembers which her hero was wont to perform— to drive an arrow straight through the hollow rings of twelve axe-heads set up in a line. Whichsoever of her suitors can bend the strong bow, and send a shaft right through the whole row of twelve, like the lost Ulysses, that man she will follow, however reluctantly, as her future lord. She has more than a lingering hope, we may be sure, that one and all will fail in a trial so manifestly difficult. They would refuse the ordeal, but for Antinous. Confident in his own powers, he hopes to succeed — he knows the rest will fail. They, out of shame, accept the test. Telemachus himself fixes the weapons firmly in the earth in a true and even line, a task in itself of no small difficulty, but which he performs with such skill as to win the admiration of the whole party. He claims the right to make trial first himself, in the hope to prove himself his father's true son. Thrice he draws the bow-string, but not yet to its right extent. As he is making a fourth attempt, sanguine of success, he meets a look from his father which checks his hand. Ulysses foresees that should his son succeed where the others fail, and so claim what they are really seeking, the royal power of Ithaca, the whole band might suddenly unite against him, and so frustrate his present scheme of vengeance. Reluctantly, at his father's sign, the youth lays down the bow, and professes to lament the weakness of his degenerate hand. One after another the rival princes in turn strive to bend it, but in vain; even Antinous and Eurymachus, notably the best among them, fail to move the string, though the bow is warmed by the fire and rubbed well with melted fat to make it more pliable. Antinous finds plausible excuse for the failure—they have profaned the festival of Apollo by this contest; it shall be renewed under better auspices on the morrow. Then the seeming beggar (who meanwhile has made himself known as their true lord to Eumæus and another faithful retainer, the herdsman Philœtius) makes request that he may try his hand upon this wondrous bow. Loud and coarse is the abuse which Antinous and his fellows shower upon him for his audacity; but Telemachus exerts the authority in his mother's house which his uninvited guests seem never quite to make up their minds to dispute when it is firmly claimed, and the weapon is given into the hands of its true owner. He handles it gently and lovingly, turning it over and over to see whether it has in any way suffered by time or decay, and brings notes from the tight-strained bow-string, "shrill and sweet as the voice of the swallow." At last he fits an arrow to the notch, and, not deigning even to rise from his seat to make the effort, draws it to its full stretch, and sends the shaft right through the whole line of axe-heads. It is the immediate prelude to the bloody tragedy which follows—

"'Behold, the mark is hit,
Hit without labour! the old strength cleaves fast
Upon me, and my bones are stourly knit—
Not as the suitors mock me in their scornful wit.

"'Now is it time their evening meal to set
Before the Achaians, ere the sun go down.
And other entertainment shall come yet,
Dance and the song, which are the banquet's crown.'
He spake, and with his eyebrows curved the frown.
Seizing his sword and spear Telemachus came,
Son of Odysseus, chief of high renown,
And, helmeted with brass like fiery flame,
Stood by his father's throne and waited the dire aim.

" Stript of his rags then leapt the godlike king
On the great threshold, in his hand the bow
And quiver, filled with arrows of mortal sting.
These with a rattle he rained down below,
Loose at his feet, and spake among them so:
'See, at the last our matchless bout is o'er!
Now for another mark, that I may know
If I can hit what none hath hit before,
And if Apollo hear me in the prayer I pour!'"

The philosopher Plato, who did not spare the poet occasionally in his criticisms, speaks of this passage as worthy of all admiration. We have here the primitive type, since worked out into countless shapes, of the "situations" and "discoveries" which abound in modern romance and drama.

Ulysses aims the first arrow at Antinous. It pierces him in the throat as he is raising a goblet to his lips, and he falls backward in the agonies of death, spilling the untasted wine upon the floor; thus giving occasion (so says Greek tradition) to that which has now become a common English proverb—"There's many a slip 'twixt the cup and the lip."* His comrades stand aghast for a moment, not certain whether the shot be deliberate or merely accidental. Ulysses sets them at rest on that point by declaring himself and his purpose. They look round the hall for the arms which usually hang upon the walls, but these have been secretly removed during the previous night by Ulysses and his son. Eurymachus, who has more plausible rhetoric at his command than the others, now endeavours to make terms. Antinous, he confesses, has well deserved his fate—he had plotted against the life of Telemachus; but for himself and the rest, now that the king has come to his own again, they will submit themselves, and pay such fine as shall amply satisfy him for the despoiling of his goods. Ulysses scornfully rejects all such compromise. Then, at Eurymachus' call, the boldest of the party draw their knives and make a rush upon him. But a second arrow from the terrible bow strikes Eurymachus through the breast before he reaches him; Amphinomus falls by the spear of Telemachus as soon as he gets within range; and while the father, backed by his two retainers, holds the rest at bay—rather, we must suppose, by the terror of his presence than the actual use of his bow—the son rushes off to find arms for the little party. Ulysses plies his arrows till they are exhausted, and then the four together continue the unequal combat with the

* Πολλὰ μεταξὺ πέλει κύλικος καὶ χείλεος ἄκρου.

spears now brought by Telemachus. The details of the work of retribution, like some of the long slaughter-lists in the Iliad, sufficiently interesting to an audience for whom war was the great game of human life, are scarcely so to modern and more fastidious readers. The hero, like all heroes of romance, performs deeds which in a mere prosaic view would appear impossibilities. Suffice it to say, that with the Goddess of Wisdom as an ally (who appears once more under the form of Mentor), the combat ends in the slaughter of the whole band of intruders, even though they are partially supplied with arms by the treacherous goatherd, who brings them from the armoury which Telemachus has carelessly left open. A graze upon the wrist of Telemachus, and a slight flesh-wound where the spear of one of the enemy "wrote on the shoulder" of the good swineherd Eumæus, are the only hurts received by their party in the combat. The vengeance of the hero is implacable; otherwise it were not heroic, in the Homeric sense. Not content with the utter extermination of the men who have usurped his palace, harassed his wife, and insulted his son, he hangs up also their guilty paramours among the women-servants, who have joined them in defiling his household gods; first, however, making them swill and scour clean the blood-stained hall which has been the scene of the slaughter. The traitorous goatherd Melanthius is by the same stern orders miserably lopped of ears, and nose, and limbs, before death releases him. We find the same pitiless cruelty towards his enemies in the hero of the Odyssey as in the hero of the Iliad. Yet the poet would teach us that the vengeance of

THE DAY OF RETRIBUTION. 115

Ulysses is but the instrument of the divine justice. Like Moses or Joshua, he is but the passionless executor of the wrath of heaven; while, still to continue the parallel, the merciless character of the retribution takes its colour from the ferocity of the age. When the aged Eurycleia, who as yet alone of the women of the household knows the secret of his return, comes down and sees the floor strewn with the bloody corpses, she is about to raise a shout of triumph. But the king checks her :—

> "Nurse, with a mute heart this my vengeance hail!
> Not holy is it o'er the slain to boast.
> These Heaven and their own crimes have brought to bale;
> Since of all strangers, from earth's every coast,
> No man was honoured of this godless host,
> Nor good nor evil, whosoe'er they knew—
> And with their souls they pay the fatal cost."

CHAPTER X.

THE RECOGNITION BY PENELOPE.

PENELOPE, far off in her chamber, has not heard the tumult, for the doors between the men's and women's apartments had been carefully locked by Eumæus, by his lord's order. Even when the nurse rushes up to her with the tidings that Ulysses himself has returned, and made this terrible lustration of his household, she yet remains incredulous. The riotous crew may have met their deserved fate, but the hand that has slain them must be that of some deity, not of Ulysses. Yet she will go down and look upon the corpses. There, leaning " by a pillar" in the royal place—like King Joash at his coronation, or King Josiah when he sware to the covenant—she beholds Ulysses. But he is still in his beggar's weed, and after twenty years of absence she is slow to recognise him. Both Eurycleia and Telemachus break into anger at her incredulity. The king himself is outwardly as little moved as ever. He will give tokens of his identity hereafter. For the present there are precautions to be taken. The slaughter of so many nobles of Ithaca will scarce be taken lightly when it is heard in the island; it must not be known abroad until he can try the temper of his subjects, and gather a loyal host around him. All traces of the bloody scene which has just been enacted must be carefully concealed; the house must ring with harp, and song, and dance, that all who hear may think the queen has made her choice at last, and is holding her wedding-feast to-day—as, in truth, in a better sense she shall. Ulysses himself goes to the bath to wash away the stains of slaughter. Thence he comes forth endued once more by his guardian goddess with the "hyacinthine" locks and the grand presence which he had worn in the court of Phæacia. He appeals now to his wife's memory, for she yet gives no sure sign of recognition :—

> "Lady, the gods that in Olympus dwell
> Have, beyond mortal women, given to thee
> Heart as of flint, which none can soften well.
> Lives not a wife who could endure, save thee,
> Her lord to slight, who, roaming earth and sea,
> Comes to his own land in the twentieth year.
> Haste, Eurycleia, and go spread for me
> Some couch, that I may sleep—but not with her."

Penelope does recognise the form and features—it is indeed, to all outward appearance, the Ulysses from whom she parted in tears twenty years ago. But such appearances are deceitful; gods have been known, ere now, to put on the form of men to gain the love of mortals. She will put him to one certain test she wots of. "Give him his own bed," she says to the nurse; "go, bring it forth from what was our bridal chamber." But the couch of which she speaks is, as she and he both well know, immovable. Its peculiar structure, as detailed in Homer's verse, is by no means easy to unravel. But it is formed in some cunning fashion out of the stem of an olive-tree, rooted and growing, round which the hero himself had built a bridal chamber. Move it?—"There lives no mortal," exclaims Ulysses, "who could stir it from its place." Then, at last, all Penelope's long doubts are solved in happy certainty :—

> "Then from her eyelids the quick tears did start,
> And she ran to him from her place, and threw
> Her arms about his neck, and a warm dew
> Of kisses poured upon him, and thus spake :
> 'Frown not, Odysseus ; thou art wise and true !
> But God gave sorrow, and hath grudged to make
> Our path to old age sweet, nor willed us to partake
>
> "'Youth's joys together. Yet forgive me this,
> Nor hate me that when first I saw thy brow
> I fell not on thy neck, and gave no kiss,
> Nor wept in thy dear arms as I weep now.
> For in my breast a bitter fear did bow
> My soul, and I lived shuddering day by day,
> Lest a strange man come hither, and avow
> False things, and steal my spirit, and bewray
> My love ; such guile men scheme, to lead the pure astray.
>
> . . . . .
>
> "'But now, since clearly thou unfoldest this,
> The secret of our couch, which none hath read,
> Save only thee and me and Actoris,
> Whom my sire gave me, when I first was wed,
> To guard the chamber of our bridal bed—
> Now I believe against my own belief.'
> She ending a desire of weeping bred
> Within him, and in tears the noble chief
> Clasped his true wife, exulting in their glorious grief.

> "Sweet as to swimmers the dry land appears,
>   Whose bark Poseidon in the angry sea
>   Strikes with a tempest, and in pieces tears,
>   And a few swimmers from the white deep flee,
>   Crested with salt foam, and with tremulous knee
>   Spring to the shore exulting; even so
>   Sweet was her husband to Penelope,
>   Nor from his neck could she at all let go
> Her white arms, nor forbid her thickening tears to flow."

When they retire to rest, each has a long tale to tell. The personal adventures of Ulysses alone (however careful he might have been to abridge them in some particulars for his present auditor) would have made up many an Arabian Night's entertainment. There would surely have been little time left for Penelope's story, but that Minerva's agency lengthens the ordinary night—

> "Nor from the rolling river of Ocean's stream
>   Suffered the golden-thronèd Dawn to beam,
>   Or yoke the horses that bear light to men."

Here, according to our modern notions of completeness, the Odyssey should surely end. Accordingly some critics have surmised that the twenty-fourth and last book is not Homer's, but a later addition. But we may very well suppose that the primitive taste for narrative in the poet's day was more simple and childlike; that an ancient Greek audience would inquire, as our own children would, into all the details of the sequel, and not be satisfied even with the comprehensive assertion that "they lived happy ever afterwards." We have therefore, in the text as it has come down to us, a kind of supplement to the tale, which, as is the case with the later scenes in some of Shakespeare's tragedies, rather weakens the force of the real catastrophe. An episode at the beginning of this last book shows us again the regions of the dead, to which the god Mercury is conducting the spirits of the dead suitors—pale ghosts who follow him, gibbering and cowering with fear, into that "sunless land." The main purpose of the poet seems to be the opportunity once more of introducing the shades of the great heroes, Achilles and Agamemnon; the latter contrasting his own miserable and dishonoured end with that of Achilles, blest above all mortals, dying in battle with all the flower of Ilium and Greece around him, and leaving a name which is a sound of glory over the whole earth. So also does he contrast, to Penelope's honour, her fidelity with the treachery of his own queen Clytemnestra; giving voice to a prophecy which has been fulfilled almost beyond even a poet's aspirations :—

> "O to her first one love how true was she!
> Nought shall make dim the flower of her sweet fame
> For ever, but the gods unceasingly
> Shall to the earth's inhabitants her name,
> Wide on the wings of song, with endless praise proclaim."

Ulysses himself has yet to visit and make himself known to his aged father Laertes, who is still alive, but living in sad retirement on his island-farm, solacing himself as well as he may with pruning and tending his orchard-grounds. The recognition scene, in which the scar left by the boar's tusk is once more the touchstone, will seem tedious, as savouring too much of repetition, to most readers of our day. But there is one point which has a special and simple beauty of its own. When Laertes seems yet incredulous as to his son's identity, Ulysses reminds him how, when he was yet a child, following his father about the orchards, and begging with a child's pertinacity, he had given him "for his very own" a certain number of apple, fig, and pear trees and vines—all which he can still remember and enumerate. The token is irresistible, and the old man all but faints for joy.

An attempt at rebellion on the part of some of his Ithacan subjects, who are enraged at his slaughter of their nobles, and which is headed by the father of the dead Antinous, fails to revive the fading interest of the tale. The ringleader falls by a spear cast by the trembling hand of Laertes, and the malcontents submit, after a brief contest, to their lawful chief.

A hint of future travel for the hero leaves his history in some degree still incomplete. A penance had been imposed upon him by the seer Tiresias, by which alone he could appease Neptune for the cruel injury inflicted on his son, the giant Polyphemus. He must seek out some people who had never seen the sea, and never eaten salt, and there offer sacrifice to the god. Then, and only then, he might hope to reign for the rest of his life in peace amongst his islanders. Of the fulfilment of this pilgrimage the poet tells us nothing. Other legends represent Ulysses as meeting his death at last from the hand of his own son Telegonus (born of his amour with Circe), who had landed in the island of Ithaca on a piratical enterprise. We may remark the coincidence—or the imitation—in the later legend of the British Arthur, who is slain in battle by his illegitimate son Mordred. The veil which even tradition leaves hanging over the great wanderer's fate is no inappropriate conclusion to his story. A life of inaction, even in his old age, seems hardly suited to the poetical conception of this hero of unrest. In the fragmentary legends of the Middle Ages there is almost material for a second Odyssey. There, the Greek voyager becomes the pioneer of Atlantic discoverers—sailing still on into the unknown West in search of the Earthly Paradise, founding new cities as he goes, and at last meeting his death in Atlantic waters. The Italian poets—Tasso, Pulci, and especially Dante— adopted the tradition. In the 'Inferno' of the latter, the spirit of Ulysses thus discloses the last scenes of his career :—

> " Nor fondness for my son, nor reverence
> Of my old father, nor return of love,
> That should have crowned Penelope with joy,
> Could overcome in me the zeal I had
> To explore the world, and search the ways of life,
> Man's evil and his virtue. Forth I sailed
> Into the deep illimitable main,
> With but one bark, and the small faithful band
> That yet cleaved to me. As Iberia far,
> Far as Marocco, either shore I saw,
> And the Sardinian and each isle beside
> Which round that ocean bathes. Tardy with age
> Were I and my companions, when we came
> To the strait pass, where Hercules ordained
> The boundaries not to be o'erstepped by man.*
> The walls of Seville to my right I left,
> On the other hand already Ceuta past.
> 'O brothers!' I began, 'who to the west

---

* The Straits of Gibraltar.

Through perils without number now have reached;
To this the short remaining watch, that yet
Our senses have to wake, refuse not proof
Of the unpeopled world, following the track
Of Phœbus. Call to mind from whence ye sprang:
Ye were not formed to live the life of brutes,
But virtue to pursue and knowledge high.'
With these few words I sharpened for the voyage
The mind of my associates, that I then
Could scarcely have withheld them. To the dawn
Our poop we turned, and for the witless flight
Made our oars wings,* still gaining on the left.
Each star of the other pole night now beheld,
And ours so low, that from the ocean floor
It rose not. Five times re-illumed, as oft
Vanished the light from underneath the moon,
Since the deep way we entered, when from far
Appeared a mountain dim, loftiest methought
Of all I e'er beheld. Joy seized us straight;
But soon to mourning changed. From the new land
A whirlwind sprung, and at her foremost side
Did strike the vessel. Thrice it whirled her round
With all the waves; the fourth time lifted up
The poop, and sank the prow: so fate decreed:
And over us the booming billow closed."
     —Inferno, xxvi. (Cary's transl.)

Thus also Mr Tennyson—drawing from Dante not less happily than he so often does from Homer—makes his Ulysses resign the idle sceptre into the hands of the home-keeping Telemachus, and tempt the seas once more in quest of new adventures :—

"There lies the port: the vessel puffs her sail:
There gloom the dark broad seas. My mariners,
Souls that have toiled, and wrought, and thought with me,
That ever with a frolic welcome took
The thunder and the sunshine, and opposed

---

 * The metaphor is Homer's, Odyss. xi. 124.

Free hearts, free foreheads—you and I are old:
Old age hath yet his honour and his toil;
Death closes all, but something ere the end,
Some work of noble note, may yet be done.

. . . . . .

'Tis not too late to seek a newer world.
Push off, and sitting well in order smite
The sounding furrows: for my purpose holds
To sail beyond the sunset and the baths
Of all the western stars, until I die.
It may be that the gulfs will wash us down:
It may be we shall touch the Happy Isles,
And see the great Achilles, whom we knew."

CHAPTER XI.

CONCLUDING REMARKS.

THE resemblance which these Homeric poems bear, in many remarkable features, to the romances of mediæval chivalry, has been long ago remarked, and has already been incidentally noticed in these pages. The peculiar caste of kings and chiefs—or kings and knights, as they are called in the Arthurian and Carlovingian tales—before whom the unfortunate "churls" tremble and fly like sheep, is a feature common to both. "Then were they afraid when they saw a knight"—is the pregnant sentence which, in Mallory's 'King Arthur,' reveals a whole volume of social history; for the knight, in the particular instance, was but riding quietly along, and there ought to have been no reason why the "churls" should dread the sight of a professed redresser of grievances. But even so Ulysses condescends to use no argument to this class but the active use of his staff; and Achilles dreads above all things dying "the death of a churl" drowned in a brook. It is only the noble, the priest, and the divine bard who emerge into the light of romance. The lives and feelings of the mere toilers for bread are held unworthy of the minstrel's celebration. Just as in the early romances of Christendom we do not get much lower in the social scale than the knight and the lady, the bishop and the wizard, so in these Homeric lays—even in the more domestic Odyssey, unless we make Eumæus the exception—the tale still clings to the atmosphere of courts and palaces, and ignores almost entirely, unless for the purpose of drawing out a simile or illustration, the life-drama of the great mass of human kind. In both these cycles of fiction we find represented a state of things—whether we call it the "heroic age" or the "age of chivalry"—which could hardly have existed in actual life; and in both the phase of civilisation, and the magnificence of the properties and the scenery, seem far beyond what the narrators could have themselves seen and known.

The character of the hero must not be judged by modern canons of morality. With all the honest purpose and steadfast heart which we willingly concede to him, we cannot but feel there is a shiftiness in his proceedings from first to last which scarcely savours of true heroism. We need not call him, as Thersites does in Shakespeare, "that dog-fox Ulysses," nor even go quite so far as to look upon him as what a modern translator terms him, "the Scapin of epic poetry;" but we see in him the embodiment of prudence, versatility, and expediency, rather than of the nobler and less selfish virtues. Ulysses, both in the Iliad and in the Odyssey, is the diplomatist of his age; and it is neither his fault nor Homer's that the diplomacy of that date was less refined, and less skilful in veiling its coarser features.

Even in much later times, dissimulation has been held an indispensable quality in rulers;* and an English philosopher tells us plainly that "the intriguing spirit, the overreaching manner, and the over-refinement of art and policy, are naturally incident to the experienced and thorough politician."† At the same time, it must be remembered that Ulysses employs deceit only where it was recognised and allowed by the moral code of the age—against his enemies; he is never for a moment otherwise than true to his friends. Nay, while the kings and leaders in the Iliad are too fairly open to the reproach of holding cheap the lives and the interests of the meaner multitude who followed them, Ulysses is, throughout his long wanderings, the sole protecting providence, so far as their wilfulness will allow him, of his followers as well as of himself.

The tale of his wanderings has been a rich mine of wealth for poets and romancers, painters and sculptors, from the dim date of the age which we call Homer's down to our own. In this wonderful poem, be its authorship what it may, lie the germs of thousands of the volumes which fill our modern libraries. Not that all their authors are either wilful plagiarists or even conscious imitators; but because the Greek poet, first of all whose thoughts have been preserved to us in writing, touched, in their deepest as well as their lightest tones, those chords of human action and passion which find an echo in all hearts and in all ages.

First, that is to say, of all whose utterances we re-

---

* "Qui nescit dissimulare, nescit regnare."
† Shaftesbury's Characteristics.

gard as merely human. There are, indeed, other recorded utterances to which the song of Homer, unlike as it is, has yet wonderful points of resemblance. For the student of Scripture, the prince of heathen poets possesses a special interest. It is quite unnecessary to insist upon the actual connection which some enthusiastic champions of sacred literature have either traced or fancied between the lays of the Greek bard and the inspired records of the chosen people. Whether the Hebrew chronicles, in any form, could have reached the eye or ear of the poet in his many wanderings is, to say the least, extremely doubtful. But Homer bears an independent witness to the truth and accuracy of the sacred narrative, so far as its imagery and diction are to be taken into account, which is very remarkable and valuable. Allowing for the difference in the local scenery, the reader of the Iliad may well fancy at times that he is following the night-march of Abraham, the conquests of Joshua, or the wars of the Kings; while in the Odyssey the same domestic interiors, the same primitive family life, the same simple patriarchal relations between the king or chief of the tribe and his people, remind us in every page of the fresh and living pictures of the book of Genesis. Fresh and living the portraits still are, in both cases, after the lapse of so many centuries, because in both the writers drew faithfully from what was before their eyes, without any straining after effect—without any betrayal of that self-consciousness which spoils many an author's best work, by forcing his own individuality upon the reader instead of that of the scenes and persons whom he represents. To trace the many points of resemblance between these two great poems and the sacred records as fully as they might be traced would require a volume in itself. It may be enough in these pages shortly to point out some few of the many instances in which Homer will be found one of the most interesting, because assuredly one of the most unconscious, commentators on the Bible.

The Homeric kings, like those of Israel and Judah, lead the battle in their chariots: Priam sits "in the gate," like David or Solomon: Ulysses, when he would assert his royalty, stands by a pillar, as stood Joash and Josiah. Their riches consist chiefly in "sheep and oxen, men-servants and maid-servants." When Ulysses, in the Iliad, finds Diomed sleeping outside his tent,—"and his comrades lay sleeping around him, and under their heads they had their shields, and their spears were fixed in the ground by the butt-end" *—we have the picture, almost word for word, of Saul's night-bivouac when he was surprised by David: "And behold, Saul lay sleeping within the trench, and his spear stuck in the ground at his bolster, and the people lay round about him." Ulysses and Diomed think it not beneath their dignity, as kings or chiefs, to act what we should consider the part of a spy, like Gideon in the camp of the Midianites. Lycurgus the Thracian slays with an ox-goad, like Shamgar in the Book of Judges. The very cruelties of warfare are the same—the insults too frequently

* Il. x. 150.

offered to the dead body of an enemy, "the children dashed against the stones"—the miserable sight which Priam foresees in the fall of his city, as Isaiah in the prophetic burden of Babylon.*

The outward tokens of grief are wholly Eastern. Achilles, in the Iliad, when he hears of the death of his friend Patroclus—Laertes, in the Odyssey, when he believes his son's return hopeless—throw dust upon their heads, like Joshua and the elders of Israel when they hear of the disaster at Ai. King Priam tears his hair and beard in his vain appeal to Hector at the Scæan gates, as Ezra does, when he hears of the trespasses of the Jewish princes.† Penelope sits "on the threshold" to weep, just as Moses "heard the people weeping, every man in the door of his tent." "Call for the mourning women," says the prophet Jeremiah,‡ "that they may come; and let them make haste, and take up a wailing for us." So when the Trojan king bears off his dead son at last to his own palace, the professional mourners are immediately sent for—"the bards, to begin the lament."§ As Moses carries forth the bones of Joseph into Canaan, and David gathers carefully those of Saul and Jonathan from the men of Jabesh-Gilead, so Nestor charges the Greeks, when they have almost determined to quit Troy in despair, to carry the bones of their slain comrades home to their native land. Sarpedon's body is borne to his native Lycia, there to be honoured "with a mound and with a column"—as Jacob set up a pillar for his dead

---

* Isa. xiii. 16.   † Ezra ix. 3.
† Jer. ix. 17.   § Il. xxiv. 720.

Rachel on the road by Bethlehem. The Philistines, after the battle of Gilboa, bestow the armour of Saul in the house of their goddess Ashtaroth: the sword of Goliath is laid up as a trophy with the priest Ahimelech, "wrapped in a cloth behind the ephod;"* even so does Hector vow to hang up the armour of Menelaus in the temple of Apollo in Troy.

The more peaceful images have the same remarkable likeness. The fountain in the island of Ithaca, faced with stone, the work of the forefathers of the nation, Ithacus and Neritus, recalls that "well of the oath" —Beer-sheba—which Abraham dug, or that by which the woman of Samaria sat, known as "the well of our father Jacob." The stone which the goddess Minerva upheaves to hurl against Mars, which "men of old had set to be a boundary of the land"—the two white stones,† of unknown date and history even in the poet's own day, of which he doubts whether they be sepulchral or boundary, which Achilles made the turning-point for the chariot-race,—these cannot fail to remind us of the stones Bohan and Ebenezer, and of the warning in the Proverbs—"Remove not the ancient landmark, which thy fathers have set up." The women grinding at the mill, the oxen treading out the corn, the measure by cubit, the changes of raiment, the reverence due to the stranger and to the poor,—the dowry given by the bridegroom, as by way of purchase, not received with the bride,—all these are as familiar to us in the books of Moses as in the

* 1 Sam. xxi. 9.   † Il. xxiii. 329.

poems of Homer. The very figures of speech are the same. The passionate apostrophe of Moses and Isaiah—"Hear, O heavens, and give ear, O earth"—is used by Juno in the Iliad, and by Calypso in the Odyssey.* "Day" is commonly employed as an equivalent for fate or judgment; "the half of one's kingdom" is held to be a right royal gift; "the gates of hell" are the culmination of evil. Telemachus swears "by the woes of his father," as Jacob does "by the fear of his father Isaac;" and the curse pronounced on Phœnix by his father—that never grandchild of his begetting might sit upon his knees" †—recalls the sacred text in which we are told that "the children of Machir, the son of Manasseh, were brought up on Joseph's knees."

Many and various have been the theories of interpretation which have been employed, by more or less ingenious writers, to develop what they have considered the inner meaning of the poet's tale. Such speculations began at a very early date in literary history. They were current among Greek philosophers in the days of Socrates, but he himself would not admit them. It is impossible, and would be wearisome even if it were possible, to discuss them all. But one especially must be mentioned, not wholly modern, but which has won much favour of late in the world of scholars,—that in both poems we have certain truths of physical and astronomical science represented under an allegorical form, imported into Greek fable from Eastern sources. This theory is, to say the least, so inter-

---

* Il. xv. 36.   Od. v. 184.   † Il. ix. 455.

esting and ingenious, that without presuming here to discuss its truth, it claims a brief mention. It may be fairest to put it in the words of one of its most enthusiastic advocates. So far as it applies to the Odyssey, it stands thus :—

"The Sun [Ulysses] leaves his bride the Twilight [Penelope] in the sky, where he sinks beneath the sea, to journey in silence and darkness to the scene of the great fight with the powers of Darkness [the Siege of Troy]. The ten weary years of the war are the weary hours of the night. . . . The victory is won: but the Sun still longs to see again the beautiful bride from whom he parted yester-eve. Dangers may await him, but they cannot arrest his steps: things lovely may lavish their beauty upon him, but they cannot make him forget her. . . . But he cannot reach his home until another series of ten long years have come to an end—the Sun cannot see the Twilight until another day is done."*

So, in the Iliad, as has been already noticed, Paris and the Trojans represent the powers of Darkness, "who steal away the beautiful Twilight [Helen] from the western sky;" while Achilles is the Sun, who puts to rout these forces of the Night.†

In contrast, though not necessarily in contradiction, to this physical allegory, stands the moral interpretation, a favourite one with some of the mediæval stu-

* Cox's 'Tales of the Gods and Heroes,' p. lvii.
† Iliad, p. 8. (Paris is said to be the Sanscrit Pani—"the deceiver;" Helen is Saramà—"the Dawn;" and Achilles is the solar hero Aharyu.)

dents of Homer, which sees in the Odyssey nothing less than the pilgrimage of human life—beset with dangers and seductions on every side, yet blessed with divine guidance, and reaching its goal at last, through suffering and not without loss. Every point in the wanderings of the hero has been thus made to teach its parable, more or less successfully. The different adventures have each had their special application: Circe represents the especially sensual appetites; the Lotus-eating is indolence; the Sirens the temptations of the ear; the forbidden oxen of the Sun the "flesh-pots of Egypt"—the sin of gluttony. It is at least well worthy of remark how, throughout the whole narrative, the false rest is brought into contrast with the true. Not in the placid indolence of the Lotus-eaters, not in the luxurious halls of Circe or in the grotto of Calypso, nor even in the joyous society of the Phæacians, but only in the far-off home, the seat of the higher and better affections, is the pilgrim's real resting-place. The key-note of this didactic interpretation, which has an undoubted beauty and pathos of its own, making the old Greek poet, like the Mosaic law, a schoolmaster to Christian doctrine, has been well touched by a modern writer:—

> " O beautiful and strange epitome
> Of this our life, while through the tale we trace
> Homeless Ulysses on the land and sea !
> From childhood to old age it is the face
> Of heaven-lost, yearning man : from place to place
> Whether he wander forth abroad, or knows
> No change but of home-nature and of grace,

> Still is he as one seeking for repose—
> A man of many thoughts, a man of many woes."

Some of the early religious commentators pushed such interpretations to extravagance; they dealt with Homer as the extreme patristic school of theology dealt with the Old Testament: they so busied themselves in seeking for mystical interpretations in every verse, that they held the plain and literal meaning of the text as of almost secondary importance. It was said of one French scholar—D'Aurat—a man of some learning, that he spent his life in trying to find all the Bible in Homer. Such men saw Paradise disguised in the gardens of Alcinous; the temptation of the chaste Bellerophon was but a pagan version of the story of Joseph; the fall of Troy evidently prefigured, to their fancy, the destruction of Jerusalem. Some went even further, and turned this tempting weapon of allegory against their religious opponents: thus Doctor Jacobus Hugo saw the Lutheran heretics prefigured in the Lotus-eaters of the Odyssey, and thought that the reckless Antinous was a type of Martin Luther himself. Those who are content to take Homer as he is, the poet of all ages, without seeking to set him up either as a prophet or as a moral philosopher, may take comfort from the brief criticism of Lord Bacon upon all over-curious interpretation—"I do rather think the fable was first, and the exposition devised after." The most ingenious theories as to the hidden

* Williams's 'Christian Scholar.'

meaning of the song are at best but the mists which the Homerists have thrown round their deity—

"The moony vapour rolling round the king."

He moves among them all, a dim mysterious figure, but hardly less than divine.

END OF THE ODYSSEY

PRINTED BY WILLIAM BLACKWOOD AND SONS, EDINBURGH.

www.ingramcontent.com/pod-product-compliance
Lightning Source LLC
Chambersburg PA
CBHW030358170426
43202CB00010B/1416